MASTERING ESSENTIAL BUSINESS SKILLS

STRATEGIES FOR TODAY'S COMPETITIVE BUSINESS WORLD

BY

DR. LUCAS D. SHALLUA

Copyright © 2024 by Global Empowerment Press Inc.

All rights reserved. This book or any portion thereof may not be reproduced or used in any manner whatsoever without the express written permission of the publisher except for the use of brief quotations in a book review.

Printed in the United States of America
First Printing, June 2024
ISBN 979-8-32-780366-4

Global Empowerment Press
4025 University Parkway, Suite 100
Winston Salem, NC 27106, USA
www.Globalempowermentpress.com

Table of Contents

INTRODUCTION 14
    The Purpose of This Book........................... 16
    How to Use This Book 17
    The Importance of Essential Skills 18

EFFECTIVE COMMUNICATION 22
    The Importance of Clarity........................... 23
    Active Listening Skills 24
    Conflict Resolution Strategies 31
    Persuasion and Negotiation Techniques 38
    Strategies for Self-Improvement 46

LEADERSHIP EXCELLENCE 52
    Understanding Leadership 53
    Developing Your Leadership Style 55
    Defining Leadership in the Modern World.... 61
    The Core Attributes of a Great Leader 63
    Inspiring and Motivating Your Team............ 70
    Decision Making and Risk Management 75
    Making Informed Decisions 76
    Mentorship and Succession 84
    Strategies for Self-Improvement 87

STRATEGIC THINKING 92
    The Essence of Strategic Thinking............... 93
    Scenario Planning Techniques 97
    Decision Making in Strategic Planning 99

Linking Strategy to Execution 103
Creating Innovative Solutions 107
Strategies for Self-Improvement 112

TIME MANAGEMENT 118
Time: Asset You Cannot Renew 119
Prioritization: Aligning Tasks with Goals ... 120
Techniques for Efficient Scheduling 124
Productivity Techniques 126
Delegation.. 128
Setting Realistic Deadlines 131
Balancing Professional and Personal Life... 136
Strategies for Self-Improvement 140

FINANCIAL ACUMEN 148
Understanding Financial Principles........... 149
Budgeting Basics 154
Investment Principles............................... 156
Cost Control Strategies 158
Economic Indicators 160
Strategies for Self-Improvement 169

PROJECT MANAGEMENT 176
Understanding Project Life Cycles 178
Effective Planning 179
Budgeting and Cost Control 183
Team Dynamics and Leadership................ 185
Quality Assurance in Projects 187
Closing Projects Successfully 193

Strategies for Self-Improvement 196
SALES AND MARKETING 204
　　Understanding the Sales Funnel 205
　　Effective Sales Techniques 206
　　The Art of Persuasion in Sales................... 209
　　Digital Marketing Trends.......................... 213
　　Customer Relationship Management......... 215
　　Creating Effective Marketing Strategy........ 217
　　Pricing Strategies for Maximum Profit 221
　　Sales Metrics and KPIs............................. 223
　　Leveraging Social-Media........................... 225
　　Negotiation Techniques 226
　　Strategies for Self-Improvement 231
ADAPTABILITY & RESILIENCE 238
　　Understanding Adaptability 239
　　The Psychology of Resilience 239
　　Cultivating a Flexible Team Culture 242
　　Strategies for Overcoming Adversity 244
　　Leveraging Failure as an Opportunity........ 245
　　Innovating Under Pressure....................... 247
　　Strategies for Self-Improvement 251
CUSTOMER FOCUS 258
　　Understanding Customer Needs................ 259
　　Building Strong Relationships................... 260
　　Implementing Customer Feedback 264
　　Empathy and Emotional Intelligence......... 267

    Measuring Customer Satisfaction 269
    Resolving Conflicts Effectively 270
    Handling Customer Complaints 272
    Creating a Customer-Centric Culture 276
    Building Customer Loyalty 277
    Strategies for Self-Improvement 284

CONTINUOUS LEARNING AND DEVELOPMENT 292

    The Imperative for Continuous Learning ... 293
    Professional Development Opportunities ... 293
    Personal and Corporate Learning Needs 297
    Staying Ahead of Industry Trends 299
    Modern Learning Techniques and Tools 303
    Creating a Culture of Learning 305
    Overcoming Barriers to Learning............... 307
    Strategies for Self-Improvement 309

ACKNOWLEDGEMENT

To my beautiful, loving wife, great partner, and long-time best friend —Dr. Dorothy Shallua has been supporting and encouraging me throughout the process.

PREFACE

Master the Art of Business Success
Are you ready to transform your career and elevate your business acumen to unparalleled heights? Discover the secrets that top professionals use to thrive in today's competitive landscape. With our latest guide, you'll gain invaluable insights into the core competencies that define true success.

Imagine confidently articulating your ideas, inspiring a team to new heights, and making strategic decisions with ease. Picture yourself managing your time so effectively that you achieve a perfect work-life balance, understanding the intricacies of budgeting and investment like a seasoned pro, and delivering exceptional customer service that builds unwavering loyalty.

Within the pages of this essential guide, we reveal the proven strategies behind effective communication, leadership excellence, and strategic thinking. Dive deep into chapters dedicated to enhancing productivity through expert time management, mastering financial acumen, and executing successful projects. Discover how to attract customers and drive growth with cutting-edge sales and marketing techniques, navigate change with unparalleled adaptability, and stay ahead of the curve with continuous learning.

Feel the surge of confidence as you apply these principles and watch your professional life transform. With actionable insights and practical advice, this guide is more than just a book—it's a roadmap to your success. Don't let the competition outpace you; grasp the tools and strategies that will place you at the forefront of your field.

Your journey to unparalleled business success begins now. Are you ready to take the first step? Embrace the knowledge and start your transformation today.

INTRODUCTION

"Mastering essential business skills is crucial for navigating complexities, driving innovation, and leading confidently. It forms the foundation for personal growth, organizational success, and adaptability in a dynamic marketplace."

Welcome to Your Leadership Journey

Leadership is not just a title or a position; it's a journey of continuous growth, learning, and self-discovery. This book is your companion on this transformative quest, designed to equip you with the essential tools, insights, and strategies to thrive as a leader in today's dynamic world. As we embark on this journey together, our overarching goal is to empower you to unleash your full potential and become a visionary and influential leader. Throughout the chapters that follow, we'll look into the core principles of effective leadership, from communication and strategic thinking to adaptability and customer focus, providing you with actionable guidance to navigate the complexities and challenges of leadership.

At the heart of this journey lies the belief that leadership is not defined by a one-size-fits-all approach but rather by a combination of individual authenticity, emotional intelligence, and the ability to inspire and mobilize others towards a shared vision. Our aim is for you to emerge from this experience with a renewed sense of purpose, clarity about your unique leadership style, and the confidence to lead with passion and integrity. Together, let's lay the groundwork for an enriching and fulfilling leadership journey.

The Purpose of This Book

This book has been meticulously crafted to serve as a comprehensive guide for aspiring and established leaders alike. *The purpose of this book is to provide you with practical insights, strategies, and valuable tools to accelerate your leadership journey.* By looking into the pages of this book, you will gain a deeper understanding of the multifaceted nature of leadership and cultivate the essential skills that are crucial for effective leadership in today's dynamic and complex business landscape. **Our goal is to empower you with the knowledge and resources you need to lead with confidence, clarity, and purpose.**

Through real-world examples, actionable advice, and thought-provoking exercises, this book aims to inspire you to elevate your leadership potential and achieve remarkable results. Whether you are a seasoned executive seeking to refine your leadership approach or an emerging leader hungry for guidance, this book's purpose is to equip you with the insight and capability necessary to thrive in the realm of leadership. Moreover, by offering a blend of theoretical concepts and practical applications, this book endeavors to bridge the gap between leadership theory and its real-world implementation, arming you with the adaptive expertise needed to navigate diverse challenges and opportunities in today's ever-evolving workplace. As you embark on this enriching journey through the contents of this book, embrace the opportunity to uncover new perspectives, cultivate growth, and unleash your full leadership potential.

How to Use This Book

In order to derive the maximum benefit from this book, it is essential to approach it with an open mind and a willingness to engage deeply with the concepts presented. The content is designed to be practical and actionable, so you are encouraged to take a proactive approach to their learning. Take the time to reflect on the ideas presented and consider how they relate to your own experiences and aspirations.

Each chapter builds upon the previous one, providing a comprehensive framework for leadership development. *Therefore, it is advisable to progress through the chapters sequentially to fully grasp the interconnected nature of the skills and principles discussed.* As you navigate through the book, keep in mind that effective leadership is not just about acquiring knowledge, but also about embodying and practicing the concepts in real-life scenarios. With this in mind, challenge yourself to think critically about how you can integrate the lessons into your professional and personal life. Remember that learning is an ongoing process, and the true value of this book lies in its ability to inspire continuous growth and evolution as a leader.

The Importance of Essential Skills

In today's fast-paced and ever-evolving business landscape, possessing essential skills is more crucial than ever. *These foundational competencies form the bedrock upon which successful businesses and careers are built and sustained.* They are the key differentiators that enable professionals to navigate challenges, seize opportunities, and achieve their full potential and make them valuable to their businesses and organizations.

Why Essential Skills Matter:

These are core competencies that are a must to any aspiring achiever especially in business and organizations. These skills help individuals climb the career ladder fast, increase productivity of their departments and are proven to bring great job satisfaction through confidence that results by possessing them.

They bring the following:

Adaptability to Change: The business world is constantly changing, driven by technological advancements, market dynamics, and global events. Essential skills such as critical thinking, problem-solving, and adaptability allow professionals to respond effectively to these changes, ensuring they remain relevant and competitive.

Enhanced Communication: Clear and effective communication is vital in any professional setting. It facilitates better teamwork, prevents misunderstandings, and helps build strong relationships with colleagues, clients, and stakeholders. Mastering communication skills is essential for conveying ideas, leading teams, and driving successful outcomes.

Leadership and Influence: Strong leadership skills are necessary to inspire and guide teams towards achieving organizational goals. Whether you are in a formal leadership position or not, the ability to influence others, motivate your peers, and lead by example is invaluable in any role.

Strategic Decision-Making: The ability to think strategically and make informed decisions is a critical skill for success. This involves analyzing data, understanding market trends, and evaluating the potential impact of different choices. Strategic thinking helps professionals to anticipate challenges and make decisions that align with long-term goals.

Time Management: Efficiently managing time and resources is essential for maximizing productivity and achieving work-life balance. Skills in prioritization, delegation, and organization ensure that professionals can meet deadlines, reduce stress, and maintain high performance.

Financial Literacy: Understanding financial principles and practices is crucial for making sound business decisions. Whether it's budgeting, financial planning, or investment strategies, financial literacy equips professionals with the knowledge to manage resources effectively and drive business growth.

Customer-Centric Approach: Focusing on customer needs and delivering exceptional service is fundamental to business success. Building strong relationships with customers, understanding their preferences, and addressing their concerns can significantly enhance customer loyalty and brand reputation.

Continuous Learning: The commitment to lifelong learning and professional development ensures that professionals stay ahead of industry trends and continuously improve their skills. Embracing new knowledge and experiences fosters innovation and personal growth.

By mastering these essential skills, professionals are better equipped to achieve their career goals, drive organizational success, and make a meaningful impact in their respective fields. This book will guide you through developing these competencies, providing practical advice, real-world examples, and actionable insights to help you succeed.

1

EFFECTIVE COMMUNICATION

"Effective communication is the bridge between intention and understanding. It requires clarity, empathy, and active listening to convey messages that resonate, build trust, and bring meaningful connections."

The Importance of Clarity

Clarity is the cornerstone of effective communication, serving as a conduit for understanding and a powerful antidote to misunderstanding. In diverse environments, where individuals bring their unique perspectives and cultural nuances to interactions, clarity becomes even more vital. When we communicate with clarity, we eliminate ambiguities that may stem from differences in language, background, or interpretation.

By doing so, we ensure that our message resonates across diverse audiences, fostering mutual understanding and unity. Imagine a team comprised of individuals from different cultural backgrounds and with varying levels of proficiency in the language of communication. In such a scenario, the ability to convey information with crystal-clear clarity becomes imperative. It paves the way for inclusive dialogue, ensuring that every member comprehends and aligns with the shared objectives. Furthermore, in cross-functional collaborations where multiple departments converge, the absence of clarity can hinder progress and lead to costly errors. Timelines may be missed, resources misallocated, and morale compromised, all due to misunderstandings arising from lack of clarity. *By emphasizing the importance of clarity, we equip ourselves with the tools to navigate the complexities of modern workplaces.* With clear, concise communication, leaders inspire confidence and trust among their teams, suppliers, and customers. Whether it's conveying project goals, outlining performance expectations, or providing feedback, clarity serves as the linchpin of effective leadership.

Clarity transcends verbal communication; it extends to written correspondence, presentations, and even body language. The use of explicit, unambiguous language, supported by contextual cues and visual aids, enhances the overall clarity of the message. This holistic approach enriches communication, fostering deeper connections and reducing the scope for miscommunication. *Thus, by championing clarity in communication, individuals and organizations mitigate the risk of conflict, enhance productivity, and cultivate an environment where diverse voices are not only heard but also truly understood.*

Active Listening Skills

Active listening is a fundamental aspect of effective communication. It involves fully concentrating, understanding, responding, and remembering what is being said. To be an active listener, one must exhibit nonverbal cues such as maintaining eye contact, nodding, and providing verbal affirmations to the speaker. Active listening also requires one to withhold judgment and avoid interrupting, allowing the speaker to express themselves freely and completely. By engaging in active listening, individuals can foster trust, demonstrate empathy, and build strong relationships.

Active listening enables individuals to gain valuable insights, understand diverse perspectives, and uncover underlying issues. It empowers professionals to identify opportunities, address challenges, and navigate complex situations. By honing active listening skills, individuals can enhance their leadership capabilities, drive meaningful collaborations, and cultivate a positive work environment.

Active listening promotes effective problem-solving, conflict resolution, and decision-making. In summary, active listening is a vital skill that contributes to creating harmonious, productive, and fulfilling personal and professional interactions.

Verbal vs Non-verbal Communication

Effective communication is not just about the words we speak; it encompasses both verbal and non-verbal aspects. Verbal communication involves the use of spoken words, language, and vocal tones to convey messages. It includes articulation, pronunciation, and the actual choice of words. *On the other hand, non-verbal communication consists of body language, facial expressions, gestures, posture, and eye contact.* Both forms of communication play a crucial role in delivering a message effectively. Studies have shown that non-verbal cues often carry more weight than verbal cues in communication. For example, a person may say 'I'm fine' verbally, but their non-verbal cues such as a slouched posture or a furrowed brow may indicate otherwise. Understanding the interplay between verbal and non-verbal communication is essential for becoming a proficient communicator. *One must learn to align their verbal and non-verbal signals to ensure consistency and clarity in their messages.*

Being aware of non-verbal cues from others can help in interpreting their true feelings and intentions, leading to better rapport and understanding. It's important to note that cultural differences can significantly impact the interpretation of non-verbal cues. What may be considered acceptable non-verbal behavior in one culture might be perceived differently in another. Therefore, it's imperative for effective communicators to be sensitive to these variations and adapt their communication style accordingly. Mastering both verbal and non-verbal communication can lead to enhanced relationships, improved conflict resolution, and greater influence in personal and professional settings.

Crafting Compelling Messages

In the realm of effective communication, crafting compelling messages is an art that can significantly influence how our ideas and intentions are received. *The ability to articulate thoughts in a clear, engaging, and persuasive manner is paramount in various aspects of life, from personal interactions to professional presentations.* A compelling message captivates the audience, evokes emotions, and motivates action. When honing this skill, it's essential to consider the context, audience, and desired outcome. Messages tailored to resonate with specific individuals or groups increase their impact and effectiveness.

Crafting compelling messages involves strategic structuring of content to ensure coherence and relevance. *It necessitates the use of powerful language, vivid imagery, and storytelling techniques to captivate the audience's attention.* Emphasizing key points, providing relatable examples, and incorporating compelling visuals can enhance the delivery of the message.

Considering the emotional and psychological aspects of the recipients aids in creating messages that deeply resonate with them. Understanding the underlying motivations and concerns of the audience allows for the integration of empathy and understanding into the message.

Empathetic communication demonstrates genuine concern and consideration for the receiver, fostering trust and rapport. Additionally, aligning the message with the values, beliefs, and aspirations of the audience enhances its persuasiveness and resonance. Crafting compelling messages entails not only delivering information but also igniting a connection with the listeners or readers, leading to a lasting impact.

The power of persuasion lies in the ability to address potential counterarguments and concerns preemptively. Anticipating objections and presenting rebuttals within the message portrays thoroughness and foresight, bolstering the credibility of the communication. Utilizing rhetorical devices, such as metaphors, analogies, and compelling statistics, adds depth and memorability to the message, leaving a lasting impression on the audience.

Crafting compelling messages mandates considering the medium of delivery. Tailoring the message to suit the chosen platform, whether written, verbal, or visual, ensures maximal engagement and reception. Effective use of formatting, tone, and timing further refines the impact of the message, increasing its resonance and persuasive effect. *Mastering the art of crafting compelling messages empowers individuals to convey their thoughts and ideas with profound impact, steering conversations, influencing decisions, and fostering meaningful connections.*

The Role of Empathy in Communication

Empathy is the cornerstone of effective communication. *It involves the ability to understand and share the feelings of another person.* When it comes to communication, empathy plays a crucial role in building trust, fostering meaningful connections, and resolving conflicts. By putting oneself in the shoes of others, communicators can gain valuable insights into different perspectives and emotions. This understanding forms the basis for establishing rapport and creating messages that resonate with the intended audience.

In professional settings, empathy allows individuals to communicate in a way that demonstrates genuine concern for the well-being of others. By tuning into the emotions and experiences of colleagues or clients, one can tailor their communication approaches to address specific needs and alleviate concerns.

The integration of empathy into communication can lead to enhanced collaboration, as team members feel valued and understood, thus driving greater productivity and job satisfaction.

Empathy is instrumental in conflict resolution. Through empathetic communication, individuals can de-escalate tense situations, acknowledge the emotions of all parties involved, and work towards mutually beneficial solutions. This compassionate approach fosters an environment of understanding and puts emphasis on finding common ground rather than perpetuating discord.

It is essential to note that empathy in communication goes beyond verbal exchanges. Non-verbal cues such as body language, facial expressions, and tone of voice also convey empathy. The ability to actively listen and respond with empathy demonstrates respect and consideration for others' viewpoints, validating their experiences and emotions.

To cultivate empathy in communication, individuals can engage in exercises and practices aimed at enhancing empathetic skills. These may include role-playing scenarios, active listening workshops, and reflective journaling to develop a deeper understanding of one's own and others' feelings and perspectives.

Empathy serves as a powerful catalyst for effective communication. Its impact extends far beyond words, enriching relationships, fostering collaboration, and paving the way for constructive dialogue. By prioritizing empathy in communication, individuals can create a more inclusive, supportive, and harmonious environment, both personally and professionally.

Conflict Resolution Strategies

In any professional or business setting, conflicts are bound to arise. Whether it's a disagreement between team members, conflicting priorities, or misunderstandings, knowing how to effectively resolve conflicts is essential for maintaining a productive work environment. *Conflict resolution strategies encompass a range of approaches aimed at managing and resolving disputes in a constructive manner. One of the key principles of conflict resolution is to address the issue rather than attacking the individuals involved.* This involves promoting open communication, active listening, and empathy. The ability to separate emotions from the problem at hand is fundamental to successful conflict resolution.

Embracing a collaborative mindset and focusing on mutual interests rather than individual positions can facilitate smoother resolutions. It's important to recognize that not all conflicts require immediate resolution; some may need time and space to de-escalate before tackling them head-on. When conflicts do reach a critical point, having a mediator, such as a manager or designated team member, can be instrumental in facilitating a fair and balanced resolution. Another valuable strategy is to seek common ground and explore *win-win solutions*. By encouraging compromise and negotiation, parties can find mutually beneficial outcomes. It's also vital to establish ground rules for respectful and constructive dialogue during conflict resolution processes. Understanding and acknowledging differing perspectives is crucial in reaching resolutions that are satisfactory to all parties involved. Post-resolution reflection and follow-up can help prevent reoccurrences of similar conflicts and foster a culture of continuous improvement. Effective conflict resolution strategies promote a positive and harmonious work environment, enhancing productivity and team morale.

Adjusting Communication Styles

Communication styles are not universal; they differ from person to person and can be influenced by various factors such as culture, upbringing, education, and personal experiences. Understanding the diversity of communication styles is essential for effective interpersonal relationships, teamwork, and leadership. *Adjusting communication styles involves the ability to adapt and tailor your approach to accommodate the preferences and tendencies of others.* It requires empathy, self-awareness, and a willingness to step outside of one's comfort zone. Adapting your communication style to effectively connect with diverse individuals and groups is a valuable skill that contributes to building rapport, resolving conflicts, and achieving mutual understanding.

One fundamental aspect of adjusting communication styles is recognizing and respecting differences in communication preferences. Some individuals may have a preference *for direct and assertive communication*, while others may value *diplomacy and tact*. By discerning these preferences, one can adjust their tone, language, and delivery to align with the expectations of the audience. Being mindful of non-verbal cues and body language is crucial when adapting communication styles. Some people may respond more positively to open gestures and expressive facial expressions, while others might prefer a more reserved and formal demeanor. Adapting your non-verbal communication to match the comfort levels of others can foster trust and create an inclusive environment.

Adjusting communication styles involves flexibility in verbal communication patterns. Some individuals may *appreciate concise and straightforward dialogue, while others may find depth and elaboration more engaging*. By gauging the feedback and responses of your audience, you can modify your speech patterns and conversational approach to better resonate with them. Similarly, adjusting the pace and rhythm of speech can enhance receptivity and comprehension in communication. Taking into account the cultural and linguistic background of your audience is also vital; accommodating differences in idiomatic expressions, humor, and formality can prevent misunderstandings and facilitate meaningful connections.

Adjusting communication styles extends to acknowledging and adapting to digital communication preferences. In today's interconnected world, understanding how to navigate various digital platforms and tools while maintaining professionalism and clarity is essential. *Whether it's email etiquette, virtual meetings, or social media interactions, the ability to adjust your communication style to suit the digital medium can greatly impact your effectiveness and influence.* This adaptation requires proficiency in written communication, multimedia literacy, and an awareness of the nuances of online interaction. Embracing digital communication trends and customizing your approach to align with the preferences of your audience demonstrates a commitment to staying relevant and engaged in the contemporary landscape.

Adapting communication styles is a dynamic and multifaceted process that hinges on attunement to the needs, preferences, and contexts of those you communicate with. By honing your ability to adjust your communication style, you pave the way for meaningful connections, constructive dialogue, and collaborative engagement in various personal and professional settings. Mastering this skill empowers individuals to bridge cultural gaps, build cohesive teams, and inspire positive change through effective communication.

Leveraging Technology in Communication

In today's digital age, technology has revolutionized the way we communicate. The advent of various digital platforms and tools has significantly enhanced the efficiency and effectiveness of communication processes. From instant messaging and video conferencing to email and social media, technology offers a myriad of options for connecting with others and sharing information. Leveraging technology in communication allows individuals and organizations to transcend geographical barriers, enabling seamless interaction and collaboration across locations. Through the use of communication software and applications, teams can engage in real-time discussions, share documents, and coordinate projects regardless of their physical proximity.

Technology facilitates the dissemination of information on a global scale, amplifying the reach and impact of messages. This level of connectivity fosters greater engagement and participation, making it possible for diverse voices to be heard and valued. Moreover, the integration of multimedia elements enriches communication by providing visual and interactive components that capture attention and convey complex concepts with clarity. Whether through webinars, podcasts, or interactive presentations, technology empowers communicators to deliver engaging and immersive experiences to their audiences.

Data analytics and insights derived from technological communication tools provide valuable feedback that can inform strategic decision-making and refine communication strategies. By analyzing metrics such as engagement rates, response times, and audience demographics, communicators gain invaluable insights into the effectiveness of their messages and the preferences of their target audience. *However, it is crucial for individuals to exercise discernment and mindfulness in utilizing technology for communication, ensuring that convenience does not compromise the depth and authenticity of their interactions.* While technology serves as a powerful enabler, it should complement, rather than replace, the human touch in communication. Ultimately, the art of leveraging technology in communication lies in striking a harmonious balance between the efficiency of digital tools and the warmth of genuine human connection, thus creating meaningful and impactful communication experiences.

Feedback: Giving and Receiving

Constructive feedback is an essential aspect of effective communication within any organization. It serves as a valuable tool for personal and professional development while also fostering a culture of continuous improvement. The ability to deliver constructive feedback in a manner that motivates and inspires growth is a skill that every leader should master. Equally important is the capacity to receive feedback with openness and a willingness to learn. Creating an environment where feedback is encouraged and valued can significantly enhance team dynamics and individual performance. When giving feedback, it is crucial to focus on specific behaviors or actions rather than making generalized statements. This approach ensures that the recipient understands precisely what they need to maintain, improve, or change.

Framing feedback in a positive and encouraging manner can help the recipient feel supported and motivated to adapt. It's essential to provide examples and context to illustrate your points effectively. As for receiving feedback, it's vital to approach the situation with an open mind and genuine curiosity. Actively listen to the feedback without becoming defensive, and ask clarifying questions to ensure a clear understanding of the message being conveyed. Express gratitude for the feedback, regardless of whether it aligns with your expectations or not. Remember, feedback is an opportunity for growth, and acknowledging the efforts of those providing it can foster stronger relationships and trust. Constructive feedback should be timely, specific, and actionable. It should also consider the individual's perspective and current challenges. As a leader, creating a feedback-rich environment involves nurturing a culture of open communication, where both positive and constructive feedback are equally valued. Regular feedback sessions, coaching, and mentorship opportunities can contribute to a more engaged and motivated workforce. In conclusion, mastering the art of giving and receiving feedback is fundamental to driving personal and professional development. It promotes a culture of continual learning, growth, and ultimately, success within an organization.

Persuasion and Negotiation Techniques

In the business world, the ability to persuade and negotiate effectively is crucial. *These skills can significantly impact your success, whether you're closing a deal, resolving a conflict, or convincing others to adopt your ideas.*

Persuasion Techniques:

Understanding Your Audience:
To persuade effectively, know the needs, desires, and concerns of your audience. Tailor your message to address their specific interests and motivations, making it more relevant and compelling.

Building Credibility:
Establish yourself as a trustworthy and knowledgeable source. Use data, testimonials, and case studies to support your arguments, enhancing your credibility and making your message more convincing.

Emotional Appeal:
Connect with your audience on an emotional level. Use storytelling to make your message more relatable and impactful, tapping into emotions to drive engagement and agreement.

Logical Argumentation:
Present clear and logical arguments. Use evidence and reason to support your claims, ensuring that your message is coherent and convincing.

Reciprocity:
People are more likely to be persuaded if they feel they owe you something. Offer value or assistance before making your request, creating a sense of obligation and goodwill.

Social Proof:
Highlight how others have benefited from your ideas or solutions. Use endorsements and testimonials to build social proof, demonstrating that your approach is trusted and effective.

Scarcity:
Emphasize the uniqueness or limited availability of what you're offering. Create a sense of urgency to prompt action, making your offer more attractive and compelling.

Negotiation Techniques:

Preparation: Thoroughly research and understand all aspects of the negotiation. Know your objectives, limits, and the interests of the other party, equipping yourself with the knowledge to negotiate effectively.

Setting Clear Goals: Define what you want to achieve from the negotiation. Prioritize your goals and identify areas where you can compromise, ensuring clarity and focus.

Active Listening: Listen carefully to the other party's needs and concerns. Show empathy and understanding to build rapport, fostering a positive negotiating environment.

Effective Communication: Clearly articulate your position and interests. Use assertive yet respectful language to convey your points, ensuring clarity and mutual understanding.

Creating Win-Win Solutions: Aim for outcomes that benefit both parties. Explore creative solutions that address mutual interests, fostering collaboration and long-term relationships.

Managing Emotions: Stay calm and composed, even in difficult situations. Avoid letting emotions drive your decisions, maintaining a rational and strategic approach.

BATNA (Best Alternative to a Negotiated Agreement): Know your best alternative if the negotiation fails. Use this knowledge to strengthen your negotiating position, ensuring you have a fallback plan.

Flexibility: Be willing to adapt your approach as the negotiation progresses. Stay open to new information and perspectives, adjusting your strategy as needed.

Closing the Deal: Summarize the key points of agreement. Ensure both parties are clear on the terms and conditions, solidifying the deal and preventing misunderstandings.

Follow-Up: Confirm the agreement in writing. Maintain a positive relationship for future negotiations, ensuring ongoing collaboration and trust.

Mastering persuasion and negotiation techniques requires practice and experience. By applying these strategies, you can enhance your ability to influence others and achieve favorable outcomes in various business situations.

Practical Exercises

Effective communication is a vital skill in both personal and professional aspects of our lives. Practicing it regularly through exercises can help individuals improve their communication abilities and build stronger relationships. Here are some practical exercises that can be incorporated into daily routines to enhance everyday communication:

1. *Mirror Communication:* Pair up with a partner and take turns reflecting each other's gestures and expressions. This exercise promotes non-verbal communication skills, emphasizing the importance of body language in conveying messages.

2. *Storytelling Challenge:* Encourage individuals to share personal anecdotes or stories within a specific time frame. This exercise enhances the ability to express thoughts coherently and engage listeners effectively.

3. *Assertiveness Role-Play:* Participants can engage in role-play scenarios where they practice assertive communication techniques, such as expressing needs and setting boundaries in various interpersonal interactions.

4. *Active Listening Exercises:* This can include activities like summarizing a speaker's message, asking open-ended questions, and

maintaining eye contact to reinforce active listening skills.

5. *Feedback Circles:* Create a safe space for individuals to give and receive constructive feedback on their communication styles. This exercise fosters self-awareness and promotes continuous improvement.

6. *Empathy Building Activity*: Engage in an empathy-building exercise where participants share experiences and explore perspectives different from their own. This can cultivate empathy and understanding in communication.

7. *Group Problem-Solving:* Encourage collaborative problem-solving activities that require effective group communication and decision-making. This exercise simulates real-world scenario and promotes teamwork.

8. *Technology Detox Challenge*: Experiment with reducing reliance on digital communication tools and focus on face-to-face interactions. Practicing unplugged communication can strengthen interpersonal connections.

9. *Conflict Resolution Simulation:* Engage in simulated conflict scenarios to practice de-escalation techniques and constructive dialogue. This exercise equips individuals with skills to handle conflicts effectively.

10. *Public Speaking Opportunities:* Offer platforms for individuals to practice public speaking, promoting confidence and articulation in delivering messages to larger audiences.

By incorporating these practical exercises into daily routines, you can develop and refine their communication skills, ultimately leading to more meaningful and impactful interactions in both personal and professional settings.

Strategies for Self-Improvement

From a self-development and improvement perspective, becoming a solver of communication problems in the business world involves cultivating specific skills, behaviors, and attitudes. Here's how you can develop yourself to effectively address each of the major communication challenges:

Cultural Differences:

- *Cultural Awareness*: Educate yourself on different cultural norms and practices. Take courses on intercultural communication or read books and articles on cultural intelligence.

- *Open-mindedness:* Practice open-mindedness by being curious and respectful about different cultures. Engage in conversations with colleagues from diverse backgrounds to learn firsthand.

- *Language Learning*: If you frequently interact with colleagues from a particular culture, *consider learning their language* to enhance your communication and show respect for their culture.

Technological Barriers:

- *Tech-Savviness*: Stay updated with the latest communication tools and technologies. Take courses or seek online tutorials to become proficient in using these tools effectively.

- *Digital Etiquette*: Learn and practice digital etiquette, such as writing clear and concise emails, using appropriate messaging platforms for different types of communication, and managing virtual meetings effectively.

- *Troubleshooting Skills*: Develop basic troubleshooting skills to handle common technical issues that may arise during digital communication.

Language Barriers:

- *Language Skills*: Improve your language skills through courses, apps, and practice. Focus on clear pronunciation, vocabulary building, and grammar.

- *Simple Language*: Practice using clear and simple language in your communication. Avoid jargon and idiomatic expressions that may be confusing to non-native speakers.

- *Patience and Understanding:* Show patience and understanding when communicating with those who have different language proficiencies. Encourage them to ask for clarification when needed.

Lack of Clarity and Conciseness:

- *Effective Writing*: Take writing courses or workshops to enhance your ability to write clearly and concisely. Practice structuring your messages logically.

- *Public Speaking*: Join public speaking clubs like Toastmasters to improve your verbal communication skills, focusing on clarity and conciseness.

- *Feedback*: Seek feedback on your communication from colleagues and mentors to identify areas for improvement.

Emotional Barriers:

- *Emotional Intelligence*: Develop your emotional intelligence by learning to recognize, understand, and manage your own emotions and those of others. Courses, books, and self-reflection can help.

- *Stress Management*: Practice stress management techniques such as mindfulness, meditation, and exercise to maintain emotional balance.

- *Empathy:* Cultivate empathy by actively listening to others, validating their feelings, and showing genuine concern for their well-being.

- **Listening Skills:**

- *Active Listening*: Practice active listening techniques such as maintaining eye contact, nodding, and summarizing what the speaker has said to ensure understanding.

- *Avoid Interruptions*: Make a conscious effort to avoid interrupting others while they speak. Let them finish their thoughts before responding.

- *Reflective Listening*: Practice reflective listening by repeating back what you heard to confirm understanding and show that you are engaged.

Feedback Mechanisms:

- *Constructive Feedback*: Learn to give and receive constructive feedback. Focus on specific behaviors, provide examples, and suggest improvements.

- *Feedback-Seeking*: Actively seek feedback from colleagues, supervisors, and subordinates to understand how you can improve your communication and other skills.

- *Self-Reflection*: Regularly reflect on your communication experiences to identify areas for improvement and set goals for development.

Generational Differences:

- *Generational Awareness*: Educate yourself on the communication preferences and work styles of different generations. Attend workshops or read literature on generational diversity.

- *Adaptability*: Practice adaptability in your communication style to meet the preferences of different generations. Use a mix of digital and in-person communication methods as appropriate.

- *Mentorship:* Engage in mentorship relationships with colleagues from different generations to foster mutual understanding and knowledge sharing.

Organizational Silos:

- *Networking*: Build relationships across different departments by attending cross-functional meetings, joining committees, and participating in company events.

- *Collaborative Projects*: Volunteer for or propose cross-functional projects that require collaboration with other departments.

- *Communication Channels*: Promote and use communication channels that facilitate information sharing across silos, such as company-wide newsletters, intranets, and cross-departmental meetings.

Remote Work Challenges:

- *Remote Work Best Practices*: Learn and implement best practices for remote work, such as setting up an efficient home office, managing your time effectively, and using collaborative tools.

- *Virtual Presence*: Develop your virtual presence by being actively engaged in virtual meetings, using video when possible, and communicating clearly and effectively in writing.

By focusing on these areas of self-development, you can become a more effective communicator and a valuable problem-solver in addressing communication challenges in the business world and your organization.

2

LEADERSHIP EXCELLENCE

"Leadership excellence is the fusion of vision, integrity, and empathy. It involves inspiring others, making principled decisions, and nurturing a culture of trust and collaboration to achieve collective success and lasting impact."

Understanding Leadership

Leadership is a multifaceted concept that has been debated and analyzed for centuries. At its core, leadership involves the art of influencing and guiding individuals or a group towards achieving a common goal. It embodies the ability to inspire, motivate, and empower others to bring out their best potential. While some may view leaders as natural-born, charismatic figures, it's crucial to understand that leadership is a skill that can be developed through learning, reflection, and practice. Effective leadership transcends hierarchical positions; it revolves around actions and behaviors rather than titles or authority.

To truly understand leadership, one must acknowledge the diverse approaches and theories surrounding this complex subject. From trait theory, which suggests that certain inherent qualities predispose individuals to leadership roles, to behavioral theories that focus on the actions and reactions of leaders, various frameworks offer insight into the dynamics of leadership. Additionally, situational and contingency theories propose that effective leadership is contingent on the context and environment in which it is exercised. By dissecting these theories, individuals can gain a deeper understanding of the dynamic nature of leadership.

Exploring different leadership styles, such as transformational, transactional, servant, and democratic leadership, offers valuable perspectives on how leaders engage with their teams. Each style brings forth unique characteristics and approaches to decision-making, communication, and conflict resolution. Understanding these styles not only broadens one's knowledge but also fosters the ability to adapt leadership strategies based on specific situations and individual challenges.

Beyond theoretical frameworks and styles, an integral aspect of understanding leadership is grasping the ethical and moral responsibilities it entails. *Leaders serve as ethical stewards, making decisions that impact the well-being of their followers, organizations, and society at large. Issues of integrity, transparency, and accountability come to the forefront, shaping the trust and credibility leaders must uphold.* By contemplating ethical dilemmas and examining case studies, aspiring leaders can fortify their ethical compass and develop a sense of social responsibility.

In essence, understanding leadership requires a comprehensive exploration of its dimensions—embracing its psychological, sociological, and ethical facets. Aspiring leaders are encouraged to look into rich literature, engage in thought-provoking discussions, and seek mentorship to expand their comprehension of leadership. Through this journey, individuals can refine their leadership philosophy, cultivate their personal values, and lay a solid foundation for the chapters ahead.

Developing Your Leadership Style

Effective leadership is a cornerstone of success in any organization. Developing your unique leadership style can significantly enhance your ability to inspire, motivate, and guide your team toward achieving common goals.

1. Self-Awareness:

Understanding Your Strengths and Weaknesses: Begin by identifying your core strengths and areas for improvement. Self-awareness allows you to leverage your strengths effectively while addressing any weaknesses.

Seeking Feedback: Regularly seek feedback from peers, mentors, and team members to gain a broader perspective on your leadership style and its impact on others.

2. Defining Your Leadership Philosophy:

Core Values and Beliefs: Reflect on your core values and beliefs that guide your actions and decisions. A clear leadership philosophy serves as a foundation for consistent and authentic leadership.

Vision and Mission: Establish a clear vision and mission for your team or organization. Communicating this vision effectively can inspire and align your team with common goals.

3. Adapting Leadership Styles:

Situational Leadership: Recognize that different situations may require different leadership approaches. Adapt your style to meet the specific needs of your team and the challenges at hand.

Transformational Leadership: Focus on inspiring and motivating your team by setting high expectations, fostering innovation, and encouraging professional growth.

Servant Leadership: Prioritize the needs of your team members, empowering them to achieve their best and fostering a supportive and collaborative environment.

4. Building Strong Relationships:

Effective Communication: Develop strong communication skills to clearly convey your vision, expectations, and feedback. Active listening is crucial to understanding and addressing the concerns of your team.

Empathy and Emotional Intelligence: Show empathy and emotional intelligence by understanding and responding to the emotions and needs of your team members. Building trust and rapport enhances team cohesion and morale.

5. Decision-Making and Problem-Solving:

Decisiveness: Cultivate the ability to make informed and timely decisions, even under pressure. Confidence and clarity in decision-making inspire trust and respect from your team.

Collaborative Problem-Solving: Encourage collaborative problem-solving by involving your team in the decision-making process. This approach leverages diverse perspectives and fosters a sense of ownership and accountability.

6. Fostering a Positive Team Culture:

Recognition and Appreciation: Regularly recognize and appreciate the contributions and achievements of your team members. Positive reinforcement boosts morale and motivates continued excellence.

Professional Development: Invest in the professional development of your team by providing opportunities for learning and growth. Supporting their career aspirations fosters loyalty and long-term commitment.

7. Leading by Example:

Integrity and Accountability: Demonstrate integrity and accountability in your actions and decisions. Leading by example sets the standard for your team and creates a culture of trust and respect.

Resilience and Adaptability: Show resilience and adaptability in the face of challenges. Your ability to navigate adversity with a positive attitude will inspire your team to do the same.

8. Continuous Improvement:

Lifelong Learning: Commit to lifelong learning and continuous improvement in your leadership journey. Stay updated on leadership trends, best practices, and industry developments.

Reflective Practice: Regularly reflect on your leadership experiences, successes, and areas for growth. Reflective practice helps you refine your leadership style and adapt to evolving challenges.

Developing your leadership style is an ongoing process that requires self-awareness, adaptability, and a commitment to growth. By embracing these principles and strategies, you can cultivate a leadership style that inspires and empowers your team, driving success and excellence in your organization.

What Do You Want to Achieve?

Setting goals is a crucial step in your leadership journey. *It provides direction, motivation, and a clear roadmap for your personal and professional growth. As a leader, it's vital to have a vision of what you want to achieve and a plan for how to get there.* Your goals should be challenging yet achievable, pushing you out of your comfort zone while still being within reach. When setting goals, consider both short-term objectives and long-term aspirations. *Short-term goals provide immediate targets to work towards, while long-term goals give you a sense of purpose and direction over an extended period.*

When defining your goals, it's essential to make them **specific, measurable, achievable, relevant, and time-bound (SMART).** Specific goals clarify exactly what is to be achieved, while measurable goals establish clear criteria for success. Ensuring your goals are achievable and relevant to your leadership development is critical for maintaining motivation and focus. Setting time-bound goals creates a sense of urgency and helps prioritize your efforts effectively.

To identify your goals, reflect on your strengths and areas for improvement as a leader. Consider what skills you want to develop, what impact you aim to make within your organization or community, and where you envision yourself in the future.

Align your goals with the organization's mission and values, ensuring that your aspirations contribute to broader objectives and priorities. By doing so, you can demonstrate your commitment to the organization's success while pursuing personal and professional growth.

Remember that goal-setting is an ongoing process, not a one-time event. Regularly revisit and refine your goals as you progress in your leadership journey. Embrace feedback and adjust your goals based on your evolving experiences and insights. Always remain adaptable and open-minded, allowing your goals to evolve as you do. Ultimately, setting meaningful and ambitious goals will empower you to chart a path towards fulfilling your potential and becoming an effective leader.

Overview of Core Leadership Skills

As a leader, it is crucial to possess a diverse range of core leadership skills that will empower you to effectively guide and inspire others. These skills encompass a wide array of competencies, from effective communication and emotional intelligence to strategic thinking and adaptability. Effective communication is fundamental in relaying your vision and goals to your team, fostering an open and transparent environment, and establishing trust and rapport with stakeholders. Simultaneously, emotional intelligence plays a pivotal role in understanding and empathizing with your team members, driving motivation, and resolving conflicts with tact and empathy. Strategic thinking entails the ability to envision the bigger picture, formulate long-term plans, and adapt swiftly to changing circumstances. Meanwhile, adaptability, a key trait in dynamic environments, enables leaders to pivot directions, embrace innovation, and thrive in uncertainty.

Possessing strong decision-making abilities, being resilient in the face of adversity, and nurturing a culture of continuous learning and development are integral components of successful leadership. These skills collectively form the bedrock of exceptional leadership and serve as the cornerstone for cultivating a high-performing and motivated team. It is imperative for aspiring leaders to nurture and develop these core skills, as they are intrinsic to achieving sustained success, fostering innovation, and navigating the complexities of modern leadership roles.

Defining Leadership in the Modern World

Leadership has undergone a significant evolution, guided by an array of theories and models that have shaped our understanding of what constitutes effective leadership. From trait theory to situational leadership, the concept of leadership has continually adapted to the changing dynamics of the modern world.

In contemporary business environments, it is essential to examine these evolving theories to discern their relevance and applicability. *The paternalistic and autocratic leadership styles, once prevalent, have given way to more collaborative and participative approaches, reflecting the shift towards inclusive and diverse workplaces.*

The rise of technology and globalization has transformed the traditional hierarchical structures, necessitating leaders to adapt and embrace a more agile and flexible mindset. The increasing focus on emotional intelligence and empathetic leadership signifies a departure from the rigid, task-oriented paradigms of the past. As organizations face complex challenges stemming from rapid technological advancements and unpredictable market disruptions, the role of a leader in fostering innovation and managing change becomes paramount. *Effective leadership in the modern world encompasses not only strategic vision and decision-making but also the ability to empower and inspire teams amidst uncertainty and ambiguity.*

The blending of virtual and physical workspaces demands leaders to navigate through the nuances of digital leadership, ensuring cohesion and productivity across dispersed teams. Understanding the evolution of leadership theories provides valuable insights into the traits and behaviors that define successful leaders today. By recognizing the historical context and adapting to the demands of the contemporary landscape, leaders can effectively steer their organizations towards sustainable growth and competitive advantage.

The Core Attributes of a Great Leader

Great leaders possess a myriad of attributes that distinguish them in the eyes of their followers. The first and perhaps most crucial attribute is *self-awareness*. Leaders who understand their own strengths, weaknesses, and emotions are better equipped to manage interpersonal relationships and make sound decisions. Alongside self-awareness, *emotional intelligence* is an essential trait for effective leadership. The ability to empathize, communicate clearly, and navigate conflicts with grace contributes to a positive work environment and fosters trust among team members. A great leader also demonstrates unwavering *integrity and honesty*. This transparency builds credibility and cultivates a culture of trust and accountability within the organization. *Adaptability* is vital in today's dynamic business landscape. Leaders who embrace change and encourage innovation create resilient and forward-thinking teams.

Possessing a *clear vision and the ability to articulate it persuasively* is paramount. Effective leaders inspire others by conveying a compelling narrative about the future. They cultivate a sense of purpose and direction that motivates individuals to strive toward shared goals. *Humility and the willingness to listen and learn from others* are hallmarks of exceptional leadership. A leader who values diverse perspectives and solicits input from team members fosters an inclusive and collaborative environment.

A great leader exemplifies a *commitment to continuous improvement and personal development.* By modeling lifelong learning, leaders inspire their teams to pursue excellence and embrace opportunities for growth. These core attributes collectively form the foundation of impactful leadership, guiding individuals to lead with authenticity, empathy, and purpose.

Building and Leading Effective Teams

Building and leading effective teams is a critical aspect of leadership excellence. A great leader understands the importance of creating a cohesive and high-performing team that can work towards achieving common goals. One of the essential elements of this process is understanding the strengths and weaknesses of each team member and effectively leveraging those to create a collaborative environment. Communication is key in this regard, as a leader must ensure that there is open and clear communication among team members to foster trust and a sense of unity.

A leader should encourage diversity within the team, embracing different perspectives and experiences that can contribute to innovative solutions and approaches. Another vital responsibility in leading effective teams is setting clear expectations and objectives, ensuring that each team member understands their role and responsibilities. It is also crucial to provide support and resources to help team members grow and develop their skills. A great leader fosters an environment where individuals feel empowered, valued, and motivated to perform at their best.

Effective delegation plays a significant role in leading teams, as it enables leaders to distribute tasks based on individual strengths and expertise, empowering team members and promoting accountability. Conflict resolution is another essential skill for a leader, as handling interpersonal conflicts within the team can prevent any disruptions and maintain a harmonious work environment.

Celebrating successes and acknowledging the efforts of the team is essential in building morale and reinforcing a positive team culture. A leader who can effectively build and lead teams not only ensures the achievement of organizational objectives but also contributes to the personal and professional growth of the individuals within the team.

Visionary Leadership

As a visionary leader, setting strategic goals is paramount to the success of your organization. Strategic goals serve as the roadmap that guides the direction and activities of a team or company. They define the long-term vision and provide a clear sense of purpose for everyone involved. When setting strategic goals, it's essential to align them with the overall mission and values of the organization. By doing so, you ensure that every action taken and decision made contributes to the advancement of the company's overarching objectives.

Visionary leaders recognize the importance of thinking big and not being constrained by the status quo. They understand that strategic goals should stretch the limits of what is currently achievable, encouraging innovation and growth. These goals should be ambitious yet attainable, motivating individuals to reach new heights and push beyond their comfort zones. Effective leaders communicate these strategic goals in a compelling and inspiring manner, igniting passion and commitment within their teams. They paint a vivid picture of the future, illustrating how the attainment of these goals will positively impact the organization, its employees, and its stakeholders. By articulating the potential benefits and demonstrating unwavering belief in the vision, leaders instill confidence and a shared sense of purpose among their teams. Moreover, strategic goals must be dynamic and adaptable to changing market conditions and internal challenges.

Visionary leaders foster an environment that *encourages agility and continuous improvement,* allowing for the adjustment of strategic goals when necessary. They remain vigilant in monitoring progress, identifying potential roadblocks, and recalibrating as needed to stay on course towards the envisioned future.

Communicating Your Vision

Communicating your vision is a crucial aspect of leadership excellence. *A leader with a clear and compelling vision can motivate and inspire their team to achieve great things.* Effective communication of the vision ensures that every member understands the direction in which the organization is headed and how their individual roles contribute to the bigger picture. To communicate your vision effectively, it's essential to use various channels and methods to reach different audience groups. Whether it's through town hall meetings, email updates, one-on-one discussions, or visual presentations, the message must be consistent and tailored to resonate with diverse perspectives. Furthermore, a compelling vision should address not only the 'what' but also the 'why.' By articulating the purpose behind the goals, leaders can ignite passion and commitment within their teams. Moreover, *storytelling is a powerful way to convey the vision, as narratives have the ability to evoke emotions and create memorable impact.* Crafting a narrative that illustrates the journey towards the vision can deeply resonate with individuals and instill a sense of shared purpose.

Incorporating feedback loops into the communication process fosters an environment of transparency and inclusivity. It allows for open discussions, clarification of doubts, and alignment of expectations. Active listening to the concerns and ideas of the team members reinforces their investment in the vision and builds a stronger sense of belonging. Lastly, embodying the vision through one's own actions and decisions is paramount. Consistency between what is communicated and what is practiced showcases authenticity and cultivates trust. In summary, effective communication of the vision involves utilizing diverse communication channels, emphasizing the *'why'* alongside the *'what,'* weaving compelling narratives, embracing feedback, and leading by example. As a leader, mastering these aspects empowers you to unite, inspire, and drive your team towards the realization of your collective vision.

Leading by Example: Ethics and Integrity

Leadership is not just about making decisions or setting goals; it's also about embodying the values and principles that guide your actions. In today's complex and dynamic business landscape, leaders are constantly under scrutiny, and their conduct sets the tone for the entire organization. *Ethical leadership is crucial in fostering a work culture based on trust, respect, and accountability.* It goes beyond adhering to legal regulations and encompasses promoting fairness, transparency, and empathy in all dealings. As a leader, practicing ethics and integrity means consistently demonstrating honesty, humility, and a commitment to doing what is morally right, even when faced with difficult choices. By leading with integrity, you inspire others to follow suit, creating a cohesive and principled team.

Ethical leadership contributes to building a positive reputation for the organization, enhancing its credibility and sustainable success. A key aspect of leading by example involves upholding high standards of behavior and consistently modeling the values and ethical principles you expect from your team. This includes being open and transparent in communication, admitting mistakes, and taking responsibility for the outcomes of your decisions. It also entails addressing ethical dilemmas with fairness and impartiality, regardless of personal interests or pressures. Integrating ethical considerations into everyday decision-making processes is fundamental to fostering a culture of integrity within the organization. Leaders must emphasize the importance of ethical conduct through policies, training programs, and recognition of ethical behavior. By providing clear guidance and support, leaders can empower employees to make ethical choices even in challenging situations.

Ethical leadership is pivotal in building long-term trust and loyalty among stakeholders, including employees, customers, and partners. As a leader, embracing ethical principles and acting with integrity not only shapes the organizational culture but also sets the stage for sustainable growth and positive impact in the broader community.

Inspiring and Motivating Your Team

Effective leaders understand the importance of inspiring and motivating their teams to achieve collective goals. By fostering a positive and engaging work environment, leaders can drive their teams to perform at their best.

1. Communicating a Compelling Vision:

Articulating the Vision: Clearly communicate your vision and the goals you aim to achieve. A compelling vision provides direction and purpose, motivating your team to work towards a common objective.

Inspiring Commitment: Share your passion and enthusiasm for the vision. When your team sees your commitment, they are more likely to feel inspired and dedicated to the cause.

2. Setting Clear and Achievable Goals:

SMART Goals: Establish Specific, Measurable, Achievable, Relevant, and Time-bound (SMART) goals. Clear goals provide a roadmap for success and help your team understand what is expected of them.

Regular Check-Ins: Conduct regular check-ins to monitor progress and provide feedback. This ensures that your team stays on track and feels supported in their efforts.

3. Empowering Team Members:

Delegating Responsibility: Trust your team members with important tasks and responsibilities. Empowering them to take ownership of their work fosters a sense of accountability and pride.

Encouraging Autonomy: Allow your team the freedom to make decisions and solve problems independently. Autonomy boosts confidence and motivation.

4. Recognizing and Celebrating Achievements:

Public Acknowledgment: Regularly recognize and celebrate individual and team achievements. Public acknowledgment reinforces positive behavior and motivates others to strive for excellence. *The rule of the thumb is to recognize and acknowledge in public, correct and reprimand privately.* Many leaders have made the mistake of correcting their team members in public. That can be very demoralizing and demotivating to many people.

Rewards and Incentives: Implement a system of rewards and incentives to recognize hard work and dedication. Whether it's a simple thank-you note or a formal award, recognition can significantly boost morale.

5. Providing Opportunities for Growth:

Professional Development: Invest in the professional development of your team by offering training, workshops, and opportunities for career advancement. Supporting their growth demonstrates your commitment to their success.

Mentorship and Coaching: Provide mentorship and coaching to help team members develop their skills and achieve their potential. Personalized guidance fosters a supportive and motivating environment.

6. Fostering a Positive Work Environment:

Open Communication: Encourage open and honest communication within the team. Create a safe space where team members feel comfortable sharing ideas, feedback, and concerns.

Building Trust: Establish trust by being transparent, reliable, and consistent in your actions and decisions. Trust is the foundation of a strong and motivated team.

7. Encouraging Team Collaboration:

Team-Building Activities: Organize team-building activities to strengthen relationships and improve collaboration. A cohesive team is more likely to work together effectively and achieve collective goals.

Cross-Functional Projects: Encourage collaboration across different functions and departments. Diverse perspectives and skills can lead to innovative solutions and a more dynamic work environment.

8. Leading by Example:

Demonstrating Passion: Show your passion and dedication to the work. Your enthusiasm will inspire your team to adopt a similar attitude.

Exemplifying Work Ethic: Model the behavior and work ethic you expect from your team. Leading by example sets the standard and motivates your team to follow suit.

9. Supporting Work-Life Balance:

Flexible Work Arrangements: Offer flexible work arrangements to help team members balance their personal and professional lives. A healthy work-life balance reduces burnout and increases job satisfaction.

Promoting Well-Being: Encourage practices that promote physical and mental well-being, such as regular breaks, exercise, and stress management techniques.

10. Continuous Feedback and Improvement:

Regular Feedback: Provide constructive feedback regularly to help team members improve and grow. Positive reinforcement and constructive criticism are both essential for development.

Soliciting Input: Seek feedback from your team on your leadership and the work environment. Use this input to make improvements and demonstrate that you value their perspectives.

Inspiring and motivating your team requires a combination of clear communication, empowerment, recognition, and support. By implementing these strategies, you can create a motivating work environment that drives your team to achieve their best.

Decision Making and Risk Management

Decision making and risk management are critical components of effective leadership. In today's dynamic business environment, leaders constantly face the challenge of making complex decisions amidst uncertainty and change. *Effective decision making involves a systematic approach that considers various factors such as potential outcomes, resource allocation, and long-term consequences.* Leaders must weigh the risks and benefits of each decision while analyzing the potential impact on stakeholders, the organization, and its strategic objectives. A thorough evaluation of available data, market trends, and competitive landscape is vital in minimizing uncertainties and making well-informed decisions.

Risk management is an integral part of the decision-making process. *Leaders must not only identify potential risks but also develop proactive strategies to mitigate and manage these risks effectively.* This requires a deep understanding of the internal and external risk factors that could impact the organization's performance and reputation. Moreover, anticipating and preparing for potential disruptions ensures that the organization can adapt swiftly to unexpected challenges.

Leaders need to foster a culture that encourages calculated risk-taking and innovation while maintaining a keen focus on managing potential downsides. Embracing a culture that acknowledges and learns from failures can lead to breakthroughs and advancements. *Building a multidisciplinary team equipped with diverse perspectives can help in elucidating blind spots and enhancing the robustness of decision making and risk management processes.*

In essence, effective decision making and risk management demand a combination of analytical thinking, foresight, and leadership acumen. It is through this strategic and mindful approach that leaders can navigate complex decisions with confidence, steer the organization towards its goals, and cultivate a resilient and forward-thinking organizational culture.

Making Informed Decisions

Effective decision-making is a critical component of successful leadership. The ability to make informed decisions can significantly impact the direction and success of your team and organization.

1. Gathering Relevant Information:

Comprehensive Research: Conduct thorough research to gather all necessary information. Utilize reliable sources and ensure you have a complete understanding of the situation.

Consulting Experts: Seek advice from subject matter experts and experienced colleagues. Their insights can provide valuable perspectives and help you make more informed decisions.

2. Analyzing Data:

Data Interpretation: Analyze quantitative and qualitative data to identify trends, patterns, and correlations. Understanding the data can reveal crucial insights that inform your decision.

Risk Assessment: Evaluate potential risks and benefits associated with each option. Consider the short-term and long-term implications of your decision.

3. Considering Alternatives:

Brainstorming Options: Generate multiple alternatives before making a decision. This allows you to compare different approaches and choose the most effective one.

Evaluating Pros and Cons: Assess the advantages and disadvantages of each alternative. Consider factors such as feasibility, cost, time, and impact on stakeholders.

4. Involving Stakeholders:

Collaborative Decision-Making: Involve key stakeholders in the decision-making process. Their input and buy-in can enhance the quality of the decision and facilitate smoother implementation.

Seeking Diverse Perspectives: Encourage input from a diverse group of individuals. Different perspectives can uncover blind spots and lead to more innovative solutions.

5. Using Decision-Making Frameworks:

SWOT Analysis: Utilize SWOT (Strengths, Weaknesses, Opportunities, Threats) analysis to systematically evaluate your options. This framework helps you understand the internal and external factors affecting your decision.

Cost-Benefit Analysis: Conduct a cost-benefit analysis to weigh the financial and non-financial impacts of each alternative. This approach helps you prioritize options that offer the greatest overall benefit.

6. Balancing Intuition and Logic:

Intuitive Judgement: Trust your instincts, especially if you have significant experience in the area. Intuition can provide valuable insights that are not immediately apparent through data alone.

Logical Reasoning: Complement your intuition with logical reasoning. Ensure that your decision is grounded in evidence and rational analysis.

7. Making Timely Decisions:

Setting Deadlines: Establish clear deadlines for making decisions. Timely decision-making is crucial to maintaining momentum and avoiding unnecessary delays.

Avoiding Analysis Paralysis: Recognize when you have enough information to make a decision. Overanalyzing can lead to indecision and missed opportunities.

8. Communicating Decisions:

Clear Communication: Communicate your decision clearly and concisely to all relevant parties. Ensure that everyone understands the rationale behind the decision and their roles in its implementation.

Providing Context: Explain the context and reasoning that led to your decision. This transparency builds trust and fosters a sense of inclusion among team members.

9. Monitoring and Adjusting:

Implementation Tracking: Monitor the implementation of your decision to ensure it is proceeding as planned. Track key metrics and indicators to assess progress.

Flexibility and Adaptability: Be prepared to adjust your decision if new information or circumstances arise. Flexibility is key to responding effectively to changing conditions.

10. Reflecting on Outcomes:

Post-Decision Analysis: After the decision has been implemented, analyze the outcomes. Reflect on what went well and what could have been improved.

Learning from Experience: Use the insights gained from each decision-making experience to enhance your future decision-making processes. Continuous improvement is essential for effective leadership.

Making informed decisions requires a balanced approach that combines thorough analysis, stakeholder input, and timely action. By implementing these strategies, you can enhance your decision-making capabilities and lead your team to successful outcomes.

Innovating from the Top

Encouraging creativity within an organization can yield groundbreaking solutions, drive growth, and secure a competitive edge in the market. *As a leader, it is crucial to promote an environment where employees feel empowered to think outside the box and explore new ideas.* This entails cultivating a culture that embraces calculated risk-taking and allows for failure as a natural part of the innovation process. Leaders can set the tone for creativity by actively participating in brainstorming sessions, championing out-of-the-box thinking, and rewarding innovative efforts. By demonstrating a commitment to creativity, leaders inspire their teams to approach challenges with fresh perspectives and to explore unconventional solutions.

Effective leaders also understand the significance of balancing structure with freedom. *Providing employees with autonomy to pursue creative endeavors while offering necessary support and resources ensures that novel concepts materialize into tangible innovations.* Fostering diversity and inclusivity within the workforce can lead to an amalgamation of perspectives and ideas, sparking unparalleled creativity. Embracing diverse viewpoints generates a rich tapestry of insights and approaches, enriching the pool of innovative ideas.

Leaders can establish platforms for cross-functional collaboration, enabling employees from various departments to share insights and co-create innovative solutions. By breaking down silos and encouraging interdisciplinary collaboration, leaders foster an environment conducive to breakthrough thinking and problem-solving. Embracing technological advancements and staying abreast of industry trends is pivotal for igniting creativity within the organization. Leaders should encourage continuous learning and provide access to cutting-edge tools and resources that enable employees to stay at the forefront of innovation. By championing creativity and innovation from the top, leaders propel their organizations toward sustained relevance, differentiation, and success in an ever-changing business landscape.

Feedback and Continuous Improvement

Leadership excellence is not solely about envisioning the future and inspiring creativity; it also involves the careful management of feedback and driving continuous improvement within the organization. Feedback is a vital tool in the leader's arsenal, providing valuable insight into the effectiveness of strategies, processes, and individual performance. Effective leaders understand the importance of fostering a culture where feedback is openly given and received, creating an environment conducive to growth and development.

Continuous improvement is the cornerstone of sustained success. Leaders must instill a mindset of perpetual advancement within their teams, encouraging them to seek out inefficiencies and actively participate in evolving solutions. This proactive approach ensures that the organization remains agile and adaptive in a constantly changing business landscape. Embracing continuous improvement fosters a culture of innovation, empowering employees to challenge the status quo and drive positive change throughout the organization.

To establish a robust feedback mechanism, leaders should implement structured processes for both *formal and informal feedback*. Regular performance reviews, team evaluations, and open-door policies enable transparent communication channels, allowing issues to be addressed promptly and successes to be acknowledged. *Constructive feedback sessions* should focus on specific behaviors, measurable outcomes, and actionable next steps, ensuring that the feedback leads to meaningful improvement. Leaders should create opportunities for peer-to-peer feedback, empowering employees to support and learn from one another.

Leaders must lead by example when seeking and receiving feedback. By demonstrating humility and resilience when receiving constructive criticism, leaders set a precedent for the entire organization. Their willingness to act upon feedback and make iterative improvements reinforces the value of continuous improvement and fosters a culture where feedback is embraced rather than feared.

In driving continuous improvement, leaders should promote a *culture of experimentation and learning from failure.* Encouraging calculated risk-taking empowers employees to pursue new ideas and solutions, even if they might not always succeed. It is through these experiences that individuals and the organization as a whole can learn, grow, and ultimately thrive.

Effective leadership is about creating an ecosystem where feedback is championed as a tool for growth, and continuous improvement becomes ingrained in the organizational DNA. When leaders prioritize feedback and continuous improvement, they pave the way for sustained success and innovation.

Mentorship and Succession

As leaders strive to shape the future of their organizations, one pivotal aspect that demands attention is the cultivation of future leaders through mentorship and succession planning. This overarching responsibility requires a strategic approach to identify and develop individuals who exhibit the potential to guide the organization forward. Mentorship serves as a cornerstone in this process, offering invaluable guidance, wisdom, and tailored support to emerging leaders. By fostering a culture of mentorship within the organization, experienced leaders can impart their knowledge and expertise to nurture the talent of tomorrow.

Mentorship facilitates a reciprocal learning environment, where mentees benefit not only from the insights and experiences of their mentors but also contribute innovative perspectives and fresh ideas, thus enriching the organization's leadership collective. By investing in mentorship programs, executives lay a foundation for a robust succession plan. These initiatives aim to systematically identify and prepare high-potential individuals for roles of greater responsibility, ensuring a seamless transition when leadership changes occur.

A well-crafted succession plan is integral to organizational longevity, enabling a smooth transfer of leadership and minimizing disruptions. Through comprehensive assessments, potential successors are identified, and targeted development plans are devised to equip them with the necessary skills and knowledge. Emphasizing diversity and inclusion in succession planning can also bring about multifaceted perspectives and a rich tapestry of leadership styles, bolstering the organization's resilience and adaptability in an ever-evolving landscape.

Simultaneously, nurturing future leaders goes beyond conventional skill-building; it encompasses instilling a deep understanding and commitment to the organization's core values, vision, and ethos. Future leaders must embody the organization's cultural fabric while propelling innovative strategies that align with its overarching mission. They should be equipped not just with technical proficiencies but with a profound sense of empathy, ethics, and the ability to lead through turbulent times.

In essence, *preparing future leaders through mentorship and succession planning is an investment in the sustainability and prosperity of an organization.* It transcends individual career trajectories, encapsulating a collective ambition to perpetuate excellence in leadership and leave an indelible mark for future generations. As the baton passes from one generation of leaders to the next, it is the efficacy of mentorship and succession planning that truly determines the enduring legacy of an organization.

Strategies for Self-Improvement

Achieving leadership excellence involves addressing a variety of challenges beyond effective communication. Here are some of the most common challenges leaders face, along with strategies for self-development and improvement to become a problem solver:

Vision and Strategy

Challenge: Developing a clear vision and strategy that aligns with organizational goals.

Self-Development Strategies:

- *Strategic Thinking:* Enhance your strategic thinking skills by studying strategic management, taking courses, and reading relevant literature. Practice scenario planning and SWOT analysis.

- *Long-term Vision:* Develop a long-term vision by staying informed about industry trends and technological advancements. Set aside time for strategic planning and brainstorming sessions.

Decision Making

Challenge: Making timely, effective decisions that benefit the organization.

Self-Development Strategies:

- *Analytical Skills*: Improve your analytical skills by taking courses in data analysis and decision science. Use data-driven decision-making frameworks.

- *Decisiveness*: Practice making decisions quickly by setting deadlines for yourself. Learn from both successful and unsuccessful decisions to refine your decision-making process.

Delegation and Empowerment

Challenge: Effectively delegating tasks and empowering team members.

Self-Development Strategies:

- *Trust Building*: Build trust with your team by being transparent, reliable, and supportive. Delegate tasks that align with team members' strengths and interests.

- *Mentorship*: Develop mentorship skills by coaching team members and providing opportunities for their growth. Encourage autonomy and support their decision-making.

Innovation and Creativity

Challenge: Fostering innovation and creativity within the team.

Self-Development Strategies:

- *Creative Thinking*: Engage in activities that stimulate creative thinking, such as brainstorming sessions, creative hobbies, and diverse experiences.

- *Innovation Culture*: Learn about fostering an innovation culture by studying best practices from innovative companies. Encourage risk-taking and experimentation within your team.

Building and Leading High-Performance Teams

Challenge: Creating and leading a high-performance team that delivers results.

Self-Development Strategies:

- Team Dynamics: Study team dynamics and high-performance team models. Apply these principles in your leadership.

- Performance Management: Learn effective performance management techniques. Set clear goals, provide regular feedback, and recognize achievements.

Building a Positive Organizational Culture

Challenge: Creating and sustaining a positive and productive organizational culture.

Self-Development Strategies:

- *Cultural Leadership*: Study how to shape and lead organizational culture. Implement initiatives that reflect your values and desired culture.

- *Lead by Example*: Model the behaviors and attitudes you want to see in your organization. Be consistent in your actions and decisions.

3

STRATEGIC THINKING

"Strategic thinking is the art of envisioning the future while navigating the present. It involves anticipating trends, making informed decisions, and aligning actions with long-term goals to drive sustained success and innovation."

The Essence of Strategic Thinking

Strategic thinking is the cornerstone of professional success, as it enables individuals and organizations to anticipate, plan, and adapt to the ever-changing business landscape. At its core, strategic thinking requires abstract and forward thinking. It involves looking beyond immediate issues and considering long-term implications, opportunities, and risks. By embracing strategic thinking, professionals can gain a competitive edge and drive their organizations towards sustainable growth and resilience.

When exercising strategic thinking, individuals are encouraged to question assumptions, challenge conventional wisdom, and explore alternative perspectives. This approach fosters creativity, innovation, and agility in problem-solving, enabling them to navigate complexities and make informed decisions. By promoting an environment that encourages strategic thinking, organizations can foster a culture of continuous improvement, adaptability, and responsiveness. Cultivating this mindset not only prepares businesses for inevitable disruptions but also empowers them to capitalize on emerging trends and market shifts. Through a blend of critical analysis and creative vision, strategic thinking equips professionals to identify new opportunities, anticipate challenges, and develop proactive strategies that align with organizational goals. Ultimately, by integrating strategic thinking into everyday practices, individuals and organizations position themselves for sustained success in an unpredictable and dynamic business environment.

Frameworks for Strategic Analysis

Strategic analysis is a critical component of organizational success, providing valuable insights into the internal and external factors that affect a company's performance. By utilizing specific frameworks for strategic analysis, organizations can gain a clearer understanding of their competitive landscape and develop more effective strategies. *One commonly used framework is* **SWOT analysis**, *which involves assessing an organization's strengths, weaknesses, opportunities, and threats.* This method provides a comprehensive overview of the internal and external factors influencing the company and helps in identifying areas for improvement and growth. *Another important framework is* **PESTEL analysis**, *which focuses on the political, economic, social, technological, environmental, and legal factors impacting a business.* This holistic approach enables organizations to anticipate and respond to changes in the external environment. **Porter's Five Forces** *is another widely recognized framework that evaluates the competitive forces within an* *industry, including the threat of new entrants, bargaining power of buyers and suppliers, and the threat of substitute products.* By applying this framework, organizations can identify strategic opportunities and threats and make informed decisions.

Scenario planning is a powerful tool for analyzing multiple potential future outcomes based on different sets of variables and events. It allows organizations to prepare for various uncertainties and create flexible strategies. Each of these frameworks offers unique perspectives and analytical approaches, providing vital information for strategic decision-making. Leaders and decision-makers must understand and leverage these frameworks to catalyze strategic thinking and foster a proactive, adaptive organizational culture.

Setting Vision and Objectives

In the journey of strategic thinking, setting a clear vision and objectives plays a pivotal role in guiding an organization towards success. A compelling vision paints a picture of the desired future state, inspiring and aligning individuals across the organization. It is a beacon that illuminates the path ahead, providing a sense of purpose and direction. The process of defining objectives that support the vision involves translating the larger strategic intent into specific, measurable, achievable, relevant, and time-bound goals. These objectives serve as milestones, marking progress towards the realization of the envisioned future. Effective vision and objectives are not mere statements; they are ingrained in the fabric of the organization, shaping its culture and informing decision-making at every level. To set a powerful vision and objectives, leaders must engage in introspective reflection, considering the core values and aspirations of the organization. This introspection facilitates the articulation of a vision that is authentic, meaningful, and capable of igniting passion within the workforce.

The process of setting objectives demands a deep understanding of the external environment and an honest assessment of the organization's capabilities. By aligning the vision and objectives with the prevailing market dynamics and the organization's strengths, weaknesses, opportunities, and threats, leaders can chart a course that maximizes the chances of strategic success. Crafting a compelling vision and precise objectives is not a one-time event but an ongoing journey. Leaders must communicate these elements effectively throughout the organization, embedding them in the day-to-day operations and empowering teams to make decisions that uphold the strategic direction.

The adaptability of the vision and objectives in response to changing circumstances is essential. Organizations must remain agile and responsive, adjusting their vision and objectives as necessary while staying true to the overarching strategic intent. The process of setting vision and objectives is a transformative exercise that has the potential to nurture a shared sense of purpose, drive, and commitment within the organization, enabling it to navigate complexities with determination and resilience.

Scenario Planning Techniques

Scenario planning is a crucial aspect of strategic thinking, allowing organizations to anticipate and prepare for various alternative futures. This technique involves the creation of plausible, challenging, and divergent scenarios to test the robustness of strategies under different conditions. The process of scenario planning begins with identifying critical uncertainties and influential driving forces that could significantly impact the organization's future environment.

One commonly used approach in scenario planning is the *'two-axis' methodology, which involves mapping two key uncertainties on separate axes to create a matrix of four different scenarios.* These scenarios represent extreme or contrasting outcomes of the identified uncertainties and enable strategists to explore potential actions and responses to each scenario. Through this process, decision-makers gain a comprehensive understanding of the risks and opportunities inherent in different future scenarios, and they can develop flexible strategies that are resilient across a range of possible eventualities.

Scenario planning also involves the development of narratives for each scenario, outlining the context, events, and implications associated with the hypothetical future. These narratives help leaders and teams envision the potential consequences of different circumstances and stimulate innovative thinking about strategic options. By engaging in scenario planning, organizations can enhance their strategic agility and adaptability, making them better prepared to navigate uncertainty and change.

An integral part of successful scenario planning is the involvement of diverse perspectives and expertise within the organization. Through collaborative workshops and cross-functional discussions, stakeholders can contribute their unique insights and knowledge to enrich the development of scenarios. This participatory approach not only enhances the quality and depth of the scenarios but also fosters greater buy-in and commitment to the resulting strategies, as individuals feel invested in the process and outcomes.

Scenario planning encourages continuous monitoring and reassessment of assumptions and external developments, allowing organizations to adjust their strategies proactively in response to emerging signals and trends. By systematically integrating scenario planning into the strategic decision-making process, organizations can become more adept at recognizing early indicators of change and leveraging them to gain competitive advantages.

Scenario planning techniques provide a structured and dynamic mechanism for exploring the complexities of an uncertain future, empowering organizations to anticipate challenges, capitalize on opportunities, and cultivate strategic resilience.

Decision Making in Strategic Planning

In strategic planning, decision-making is a critical process that shapes the direction and success of an organization. *This process involves analyzing various alternatives and choosing the best course of action to achieve long-term objectives.* Effective decision-making in strategic planning requires a structured approach that integrates data-driven analysis, stakeholder input, and future-oriented thinking. At its core, this process involves identifying key issues and opportunities, assessing risks and benefits, and evaluating potential outcomes.

One of the fundamental aspects of decision-making in strategic planning is the consideration of different scenarios and their potential impact on the organization's goals. By envisioning various possible futures, decision-makers can prepare for uncertainty and develop robust strategies that are adaptive and resilient. Strategic planners must be mindful of the interconnected nature of decisions and their implications across different areas of the organization. This holistic perspective enables a comprehensive understanding of the strategic landscape and facilitates the alignment of decisions with overarching goals.

Effective decision-making in strategic planning involves active engagement with diverse perspectives and expertise within the organization. By fostering collaborative discussions and harnessing collective intelligence, decision-makers can leverage the full spectrum of insights and innovative ideas. *This inclusive approach not only enriches the decision-making process but also cultivates a culture of ownership and commitment among stakeholders, enhancing the implementation of chosen strategies.*

Embracing technological advancements can augment the decision-making process by providing access to real-time data, predictive analytics, and simulation tools that enable scenario testing and informed decision-making. These technological capabilities empower strategic planners to make evidence-based decisions and adapt their strategies in rapidly changing environments.

Successful decision-making in strategic planning necessitates continuous reflection and adaptation. As strategies are implemented, it is crucial to monitor their progress, evaluate their impact, and adjust course as necessary. This iterative approach acknowledges that strategic planning is an ongoing, evolving process, and that flexibility and agility are indispensable qualities for effective decision-making. By maintaining a dynamic mindset and learning from both successes and setbacks, organizations can refine their strategies and enhance their capacity to navigate complex landscapes with clarity and purpose.

Leveraging Technology

Organizations are constantly seeking ways to utilize technological advancements to differentiate themselves from competitors and achieve long-term success. We will explore how businesses can harness technology to drive strategic initiatives and propel their growth.

First and foremost, technology serves as a catalyst for innovation and creativity. By embracing cutting-edge tools and systems, companies can streamline operations, enhance product development processes, and create unique value propositions for their customers. From implementing advanced analytics for market insights to utilizing artificial intelligence for predictive modeling, technology empowers organizations to stay ahead of the curve in an increasingly competitive marketplace.

The integration of digital platforms and solutions enables businesses to optimize their strategic decision-making processes. Through the use of data-driven algorithms and real-time monitoring capabilities, leaders can make well-informed choices that align with their long-term goals. Whether it's leveraging machine learning algorithms for demand forecasting or deploying sophisticated CRM systems to personalize customer experiences, technology provides unparalleled opportunities for strategic decision support.

Technology plays a pivotal role in enhancing operational efficiency and agility, which are essential components of strategic success. Cloud computing, automation, and IoT (Internet of Things) offer scalable and flexible infrastructures that enable businesses to adapt to changing market dynamics swiftly. This adaptability not only fosters resilience but also positions organizations to capitalize on emerging opportunities and respond proactively to potential threats.

The advancements in communication and collaboration technologies have redefined the way teams work together, breaking down geographical barriers and bringing global connectivity. Remote team management tools, video conferencing platforms, and virtual reality environments are revolutionizing the concept of teamwork, enabling organizations to tap into diverse talent pools and operate seamlessly across borders.

Overall, the strategic significance of technology cannot be overstated. By leveraging technological innovations effectively, businesses can enhance their competitive positioning, drive sustainable growth, and navigate complexities with confidence. Embracing a forward-looking approach to technology adoption is essential for remaining at the forefront of the evolving business landscape.

Linking Strategy to Execution

Strategic thinking is an essential foundation for any organization's success, but without effective execution, strategies remain mere ideas on paper. *The process of linking strategy to execution is critical in translating strategic plans into tangible results.* This involves aligning organizational resources, processes, and people with the strategic goals to ensure that the envisioned future becomes a reality. The successful execution of a strategy requires a clear roadmap, effective communication, and robust project management. It involves breaking down the strategic plan into actionable initiatives, assigning responsibilities, and establishing clear timelines. Moreover, it necessitates the cultivation of a culture that promotes ownership, accountability, and adaptability. Modern businesses understand the importance of agility in executing strategies, given the dynamic nature of markets and competitive landscapes. They seek to adopt lean and agile methodologies which enable them to respond swiftly to opportunities and challenges.

The integration of technology plays a pivotal role in streamlining execution processes. Organizations are leveraging digital tools for project management, performance tracking, and real-time reporting to ensure that the execution stays on course. The alignment of individual and team objectives with the overarching strategic direction is crucial for successful strategy execution. Leaders at all levels play a vital role in cascading the strategic vision, motivating teams, and providing the necessary resources and support. An organizational structure that fosters collaboration, innovation, and transparent communication greatly facilitates the execution of strategies. Successful companies recognize the need for continuous evaluation and feedback loops to monitor progress and make strategic adjustments as required. This iterative approach allows organizations to adapt to changing circumstances, mitigate risks, and capitalize on emerging opportunities.

Monitoring, Evaluation, and Strategic Adjustment

As the strategic plan is executed, it is crucial to monitor its progress and constantly evaluate its impact on the organization's overall goals. *Monitoring involves tracking key performance indicators (KPIs) and milestones to assess whether the strategic initiatives are on track.* It also entails collecting relevant data and feedback from various stakeholders to gauge the effectiveness of the implemented strategies. This information serves as the foundation for the evaluation process.

Evaluation encompasses a comprehensive analysis of the strategy's outcomes, both quantitative and qualitative, against the predefined targets. It involves assessing the actual results achieved and identifying any gaps or deviations from the original plan. The aim is to determine the extent to which the strategy is contributing to the organization's success. Through this evaluative process, organizations can gain insights into what aspects of the strategy are working well and where adjustments may be necessary. Successful strategic adjustments are informed by a thorough understanding of the strengths and weaknesses of the current approach. This requires a willingness to adapt and make changes based on the evaluation findings. It's important to set clear criteria for when adjustments are warranted, such as shifts in market conditions, emerging opportunities, or unanticipated obstacles. Strategic adjustment involves revisiting the strategic plan, reassessing priorities, and making modifications to ensure alignment with the evolving business landscape. It may involve reallocation of resources, restructuring of processes, or even redefining the strategic direction. Moreover, strategic adjustment is an opportunity for organizational learning and improvement. By reflecting on past experiences and integrating new insights, organizations can enhance their strategic capabilities and resilience. This iterative process fosters agility and responsiveness, enabling the organization to stay competitive and agile in dynamic environments.

Effective communication is vital during the strategic adjustment phase. Clear and transparent communication helps in conveying the rationale behind the adjustments to various stakeholders, garnering their support, and ensuring a unified effort towards the refined strategic direction.

Monitoring, evaluation, and strategic adjustment are integral components of the strategic management process. They provide the necessary mechanisms for continuous improvement, agility, and adaptability, ultimately leading to sustained organizational success.

Creating Innovative Solutions

Innovation is a key component of strategic thinking, enabling organizations to stay competitive and adapt to changing environments. As a leader, encouraging a culture of creativity and developing innovative solutions is essential for long-term success. Let us explore strategies for creating innovative solutions, offering practical insights and techniques to enhance the strategic thinking and problem-solving skills.

1. Encouraging a Creative Environment:

Open Communication: Create an atmosphere where team members feel comfortable sharing their ideas and opinions without fear of criticism. Open communication encourages creativity and collaboration.

Diverse Perspectives: Promote diversity within your team to bring a wide range of perspectives and experiences. Diverse teams are more likely to generate innovative ideas and solutions.

2. Embracing a Growth Mindset:

Encouraging Experimentation: Encourage your team to experiment and take calculated risks. Innovation often comes from trying new approaches and learning from failures.

Learning from Failure: View failures as learning opportunities rather than setbacks. Analyze what went wrong and use those insights to improve future efforts.

3. Problem Identification and Definition:

Understanding the Problem: Clearly define the problem you are trying to solve. A thorough understanding of the issue is essential for developing effective solutions.

Root Cause Analysis: Use techniques like the **5 Whys or Fishbone Diagram** to identify the root cause of the problem. Addressing the underlying issue leads to more sustainable solutions.

4. Brainstorming Techniques:

Traditional Brainstorming: Gather your team to generate a wide range of ideas in a collaborative setting. Encourage free thinking and avoid immediate criticism of ideas.

Mind Mapping: Use mind maps to visually organize ideas and explore different aspects of the problem. This technique helps to identify connections and generate new insights.

SCAMPER Method: Apply the SCAMPER technique (*Substitute, Combine, Adapt, Modify, Put to another use, Eliminate, and Reverse*) to think creatively about existing processes or products.

5. Design Thinking:

Empathy: Start by understanding the needs and perspectives of the end-users. Empathy is crucial for designing solutions that truly address user needs.

Define: Clearly articulate the problem based on user insights. A well-defined problem statement guides the innovation process.

Ideate: Generate a wide range of ideas and potential solutions. Encourage creative thinking and exploration of unconventional approaches.

Prototype: Develop simple prototypes of your ideas to test their feasibility. Prototyping allows you to quickly iterate and refine solutions based on feedback.

Test: Validate your prototypes with real users. Gather feedback and make necessary adjustments to improve the solution.

6. Leveraging Technology:

Staying Updated: Keep abreast of the latest technological trends and advancements. Technology can provide new tools and methods for solving problems and creating innovative solutions.

Digital Tools: Utilize digital tools and software to facilitate collaboration, idea generation, and project management. Tools like collaborative platforms, data analytics, and simulation software can enhance the innovation process.

7. Cross-Functional Collaboration:

Breaking Silos: Encourage collaboration across different departments and functions. Cross-functional teams bring diverse expertise and perspectives, leading to more comprehensive solutions.

Knowledge Sharing: Create opportunities for knowledge sharing and cross-pollination of ideas. Regular inter-departmental meetings and collaborative projects can foster innovation.

8. Implementing and Scaling Innovations:

Pilot Programs: Start with pilot programs to test innovative solutions on a small scale. Piloting allows you to refine the solution before full-scale implementation.

Scalability: Consider the scalability of your innovative solutions. Plan for resources, infrastructure, and processes needed to scale successful innovations.

9. Cultivating an Innovative Culture:

Rewarding Innovation: Recognize and reward innovative efforts and successes. Acknowledging creative contributions reinforces the importance of innovation.

Continuous Improvement: Promote a culture of continuous improvement where innovation is an ongoing priority. Regularly review and update processes to incorporate new ideas and technologies.

10. Reflecting and Learning:

Post-Innovation Analysis: After implementing innovative solutions, analyze the outcomes and gather feedback. Reflect on what worked well and what could be improved.

Learning and Adapting: Use insights from each innovation process to enhance future efforts. Continuous learning and adaptation are key to sustaining innovation.

Creating innovative solutions requires a combination of creativity, collaboration, and strategic thinking. By implementing these strategies, you can foster a culture of innovation and lead your team to develop groundbreaking solutions.

Strategies for Self-Improvement

Strategic thinking is a critical skill for leaders, involving the ability to anticipate future trends, make informed decisions, and create long-term plans that align with organizational goals. Here are the top five strategic thinking challenges and how to become a problem solver through self-development and improvement:

Anticipating Future Trends

Challenge: Keeping up with rapid changes in the market, technology, and industry to anticipate future trends and disruptions.

Self-Development Strategies:

Continuous Learning:

- *Stay Informed*: Regularly read industry reports, attend conferences, and follow thought leaders. Subscribe to relevant journals and newsletters.

- *Education*: Enroll in courses on emerging trends, technological advancements, and market analysis.

Scenario Planning:

- *Develop Scenarios*: Practice developing different future scenarios based on current data and trends. This helps in anticipating possible futures and preparing for them.

- *Workshops*: Participate in or organize scenario planning workshops with your team to collaboratively anticipate and prepare for future challenges.

Networking:

- *Industry Connections*: Build a network of contacts in your industry. Regularly engage with them to gain insights and share knowledge about emerging trends.

- *Mentorship:* Seek mentors who have a strong track record in strategic foresight and learn from their experiences.

Balancing Short-term and Long-term Goals

Challenge: Balancing the need to achieve short-term results with the pursuit of long-term strategic goals.

Self-Development Strategies:

Time Management:

- *Prioritization*: Use prioritization techniques, such as the Eisenhower Matrix, to balance urgent and important tasks with long-term strategic initiatives.

- *Time Allocation*: Allocate specific time slots for strategic planning and long-term goal setting, ensuring they are not overshadowed by immediate tasks.

Goal Setting:

- *SMART Goals*: Set SMART (Specific, Measurable, Achievable, Relevant, Time-bound) goals for both short-term and long-term objectives.
- *Review and Adjust*: Regularly review progress toward goals and adjust plans as needed to ensure alignment with the strategic vision.

Making Data-Driven Decisions

Challenge: Utilizing data effectively to inform strategic decisions.

Self-Development Strategies:

Data Literacy:

- *Training:* Take courses on data analysis, statistics, and business analytics to enhance your ability to interpret and use data.
- *Tools Proficiency*: Learn to use data analysis tools and software that can help in making informed decisions.

Critical Thinking:

- *Analyze Trends*: Practice analyzing data trends and patterns to extract actionable insights.

- *Bias Awareness*: Be aware of cognitive biases that can affect data interpretation and decision-making.

Data-Driven Culture:

- *Promote Data* Use: Encourage a data-driven culture within your team by emphasizing the importance of data in decision-making processes.

- *Collaborate with Analysts*: Work closely with data analysts to understand the implications of data insights on strategic planning.

Innovative Problem Solving

Challenge: Generating creative and innovative solutions to complex problems.

Self-Development Strategies:

Creative Thinking:

- *Brainstorming*: Regularly engage in brainstorming sessions to generate new ideas and solutions. Encourage thinking outside the box.

- *Diverse Experiences*: Expose yourself to diverse experiences and fields to broaden your perspective and inspire creativity.

Design Thinking:

- *Training:* Learn and apply design thinking methodologies to approach problems from a user-centric perspective and develop innovative solutions.
- *Prototyping:* Practice rapid prototyping and iteration to test and refine ideas quickly.

Risk-Taking:

- *Calculated Risks*: Develop a comfort level with taking calculated risks. Analyze potential outcomes and prepare contingency plans.
- *Failure Learning*: Embrace failures as learning opportunities. Reflect on what went wrong and how to improve in future attempts.

Building Strategic Relationships

Challenge: Developing and maintaining strategic relationships that can support long-term goals.

Self-Development Strategies:

Networking Skills:

- *Active Networking*: Attend industry events, join professional associations, and participate in networking activities to build a strong professional network.
- *Follow-up*: Maintain relationships by following up with contacts regularly and offering value, such as sharing relevant information or opportunities.

Collaboration:

- *Cross-Functional Teams*: Engage in cross-functional projects to build relationships across different areas of the organization.
- *Partnerships:* Seek out and develop strategic partnerships with external organizations that align with your long-term goals.

By focusing on these self-development strategies, you can enhance your strategic thinking capabilities and become a more effective problem solver, positioning yourself for leadership excellence.

4

TIME MANAGEMENT

"Time management is the craft of balancing priorities and maximizing productivity. It involves making deliberate choices and disciplined actions to transform fleeting moments into meaningful accomplishments and enduring success."

Time: Asset You Cannot Renew

Time, the most precious and finite resource available to us, is a currency that cannot be replenished. In both our personal and professional lives, the way in which we manage this invaluable asset can ultimately determine our success or failure. It is important to acknowledge the profound impact that effective time management has on achieving goals and fulfilling aspirations. Understanding the finite nature of time serves as a reality check, compelling individuals to reassess their priorities and make conscious decisions about how they allocate this limited resource.

Every moment spent is an investment in one aspect of life or another, whether it's furthering professional ambitions, nurturing personal relationships, pursuing hobbies, or self-improvement endeavors. Recognizing the value of time encourages individuals to make deliberate choices, ensuring that they align their actions with their long-term objectives. This awareness encourages a heightened sense of accountability and responsibility, prompting individuals to evaluate whether their current activities are truly propelling them towards their desired destinations.

Comprehending the scarcity of time provides the impetus for individuals to optimize their schedules, eliminate time-wasting habits, and focus solely on what is truly meaningful and aligned with their overarching purpose. It also instills in them a greater appreciation for every passing moment, driving them to infuse each second with purpose and intentionality.

Prioritization: Aligning Tasks with Goals

The ability to prioritize tasks is crucial for personal and professional success. *Without effective prioritization, individuals often find themselves overwhelmed by an ever-growing to-do list, leading to stress, burnout, and decreased productivity.* Prioritization involves aligning tasks with overarching goals, ensuring that time and resources are allocated to activities that contribute the most value. The first step in prioritization is to clearly define your goals and objectives.

By understanding what you want to accomplish, you can identify the tasks and activities that will support these aspirations. Once your goals are established, it's essential to evaluate the importance and urgency of each task. This evaluation allows you to categorize tasks based on their significance and the timeframe within which they need to be completed.

Prioritizing tasks that are aligned with your long-term objectives ensures that your efforts are directed towards meaningful outcomes. Additionally, it is important to consider the potential impact of each task on your overall goals. Some tasks may have a higher strategic significance, contributing directly to your mission or vision, while others may be more routine and operational. By aligning tasks with your larger objectives, you can ensure that your daily activities propel you towards desired outcomes. Prioritization requires a level of flexibility. As circumstances change, so too should your priorities. Adapting to new information and adjusting task lists accordingly enables you to remain nimble and responsive. This adaptability ensures that you are always working on the most relevant and impactful tasks.

Effective prioritization also involves managing expectations, both with yourself and with others. By communicating clearly about your priorities and the rationale behind them, you can set realistic expectations and avoid overcommitting. It's essential to regularly review and reassess your priorities. As new opportunities arise or circumstances shift, your task list may need to be updated to reflect these changes. Regular reflection ensures that you stay focused on what matters most and makes adjustments as needed. In conclusion, prioritization is a skill that empowers individuals to make intentional choices about where to invest their time and energy. By aligning tasks with overarching goals, evaluating their importance and impact, remaining flexible, managing expectations, and periodically reviewing priorities, individuals can effectively navigate their day-to-day responsibilities while staying true to their larger objectives.

Effective prioritization is essential for managing time and achieving strategic goals. By identifying and focusing on high-impact activities, you can ensure that your efforts are aligned with your most important objectives.

Key Techniques to Prioritization

1. Identifying Priorities:

Eisenhower Matrix: Use the Eisenhower Matrix to categorize tasks into four quadrants: urgent and important, important but not urgent, urgent but not important, and neither urgent nor important. Focus on tasks that fall into the urgent and important quadrant first.

	Urgent	Not Urgent
Important	1 DO	2 SCHEDULE
Not Important	3 DELEGATE	4 DELETE

SMART Goals: Set Specific, Measurable, Achievable, Relevant, and Time-bound goals. Clear goals help you identify what needs to be prioritized to achieve desired outcomes.

2. Focusing on High-Impact Activities:

Pareto Principle: Apply the Pareto Principle (80/20 rule) to focus on the 20% of tasks that generate 80% of the results. Prioritize activities that have the highest impact on your goals.

Task Breakdown: Break down large projects into smaller, manageable tasks. Prioritize these tasks based on their importance and deadlines to ensure steady progress.

3. Time Blocking:

Scheduling Time: Allocate specific blocks of time for high-priority tasks. Time blocking helps you dedicate uninterrupted periods to focus on important activities.

Avoiding Multitasking: Focus on one task at a time to improve efficiency and reduce errors. Multitasking can lead to decreased productivity and lower quality of work.

4. Regular Review:

Daily and Weekly Reviews: Conduct regular reviews of your tasks and priorities. Adjust your schedule as needed to accommodate changing priorities and deadlines.

Progress Tracking: Use tools like to-do lists, planners, or digital apps to track your progress and stay organized.

Techniques for Efficient Scheduling

Efficient scheduling is essential for effective time management. Individuals and organizations are constantly juggling numerous tasks and commitments. Without a structured approach to scheduling, it's easy to become overwhelmed and lose sight of priorities. Fortunately, there are various tools and techniques that can significantly enhance one's ability to manage time effectively. One of the most popular scheduling tools is the electronic calendar, which allows users to input and organize their appointments, deadlines, and other time-bound tasks. Platforms such as Google Calendar, Microsoft Outlook, and Apple's iCal provide features for setting reminders, color-coding events, and sharing schedules with colleagues or family members. These digital calendars facilitate seamless coordination and help individuals stay on top of their commitments.

Another valuable technique for efficient scheduling is the use of time-blocking. This method involves allocating specific time slots for different types of tasks, whether it's responding to emails, working on a project, or attending meetings. By proactively designating time for each activity, individuals can maintain focus and minimize the likelihood of procrastination. Additionally, time-blocking enables individuals to visualize their daily workload and allocate sufficient time for high-priority tasks.

Leveraging project management software can streamline the scheduling process, especially for individuals handling complex, multi-stage projects. Platforms like Asana, Trello, and Monday.com offer features for creating timelines, setting milestones, and assigning tasks to team members. These tools enable users to track project progress, identify potential bottlenecks, and adjust schedules accordingly, ensuring that deadlines are met and resources are allocated optimally.

In addition to digital tools, traditional methods such as the use of planners and to-do lists remain highly effective for many individuals. Writing down tasks and deadlines can aid in visualizing the scope of one's responsibilities and provide a sense of accomplishment upon completion. While electronic solutions are convenient, some people find satisfaction in physically crossing off completed items on a list or writing down their plans in a tangible format.

The key to efficient scheduling lies in finding a system that aligns with an individual's preferences and work style. Whether it's embracing digital calendars, adopting time-blocking strategies, utilizing project management software, or sticking to traditional pen-and-paper methods, the goal is to create a scheduling framework that promotes productivity, reduces stress, and enables individuals to make the most of their time.

Productivity Techniques

Maximizing productivity is crucial for effective time management. By implementing proven productivity techniques, you can enhance your efficiency, reduce stress, and achieve your goals more effectively. This sub-chapter explores various techniques to boost productivity in your daily work routine.

1. Pomodoro Technique:

Work in Intervals: Use the Pomodoro Technique to work in focused intervals (typically 25 minutes) followed by short breaks. This method helps maintain concentration and prevents burnout.

Frequent Breaks: Take regular breaks to rest and recharge. Short breaks improve overall productivity and mental clarity.

2. Task Batching:

Grouping Similar Tasks: Batch similar tasks together to minimize context switching and improve efficiency. For example, set aside specific times for responding to emails, making phone calls, or conducting meetings.

Dedicated Focus Periods: Allocate dedicated periods for deep work on complex tasks. Reduce distractions during these periods to enhance focus and productivity.

3. Automation and Delegation:

Leveraging Technology: Use automation tools and software to handle repetitive tasks. Automation frees up time for more strategic activities.

Delegating Tasks: Delegate tasks to team members or colleagues when appropriate. Effective delegation allows you to focus on higher-priority tasks and empowers your team.

4. Minimizing Distractions:

Creating a Distraction-Free Workspace: Set up a workspace that minimizes interruptions and distractions. Use noise-canceling headphones, close unnecessary tabs, and set boundaries with colleagues during focus periods.

Limiting Digital Distractions: Turn off non-essential notifications on your devices. Schedule specific times to check emails and social media.

Delegation

Delegation is essential skill since it empowers others to free up your time. It is a vital skill for any leader seeking to optimize their time and focus on strategic priorities. By effectively delegating tasks, leaders can empower their team members, enabling growth, and create a more efficient work environment. *Successful delegation involves not just assigning tasks but also providing the necessary authority, resources, and support to ensure that the tasks are completed effectively.* It is about entrusting individuals with responsibilities, allowing them to showcase their abilities and develop new skills.

Effective delegation is not only about freeing up time for oneself but also about bringing a sense of ownership and accountability among team members. To delegate effectively, it's essential to recognize each team member's strengths, weaknesses, and professional development goals. This understanding enables leaders to tailor delegated tasks to align with individual growth opportunities while ensuring successful outcomes. Clear communication regarding expectations, timelines, and desired outcomes is paramount in the delegation process. It helps in setting a common understanding and ensures clarity, which minimizes the need for follow-ups and corrections.

However, while delegation can be empowering, it also requires trust and a willingness to accept that not everything will be done exactly as one might do it. *Leaders must resist the urge to micromanage and allow their team members the freedom to complete tasks in their own way, which can lead to innovative approaches and fresh perspectives.*

Effective delegation involves continuous feedback and acknowledgment of the efforts and achievements of the delegated tasks, fostering a culture of recognition and appreciation. Recognizing and celebrating successful outcomes enhances motivation and encourages team members to take on new challenges. It's important to remember that mistakes may happen when tasks are delegated, and it's crucial to view these as learning opportunities for both the leader and the team member. Through responsible delegation, leaders can inspire and empower their teams, creating an environment where everyone thrives, resulting in increased productivity and performance.

Procrastination and Distractions

In a demanding work environment, avoiding procrastination and minimizing distractions are essential skills for effective time management. Procrastination, often characterized by the delay of important tasks, can significantly impede productivity and result in unnecessary stress. To combat procrastination, individuals should cultivate self-awareness and identify their underlying reasons for avoidance. Understanding personal triggers and tendencies is the first step towards implementing strategies to overcome procrastination.

Minimizing distractions is equally crucial in optimizing focus and productivity. In today's digital age, constant notifications, emails, and social media platforms can disrupt workflow and diminish concentration. Employing proactive measures such as setting specific times for checking emails or silencing notifications during critical tasks can substantially reduce distractions. Creating a conducive work environment by minimizing clutter and utilizing noise-cancelling headphones can further enhance concentration.

Practicing mindfulness techniques and incorporating regular breaks into the workday can help mitigate the impact of distractions. Mindfulness encourages individuals to maintain present-moment awareness and promotes intentional focus, reducing the allure of procrastination and external disruptions. Intermittent breaks can rejuvenate mental energy and serve as an opportunity to recalibrate concentration levels. By embracing these practices, individuals can fortify their ability to remain attentive amidst potential distractions and propel themselves towards accomplishing their objectives with greater efficiency.

Setting Realistic Deadlines

Deadlines are an integral aspect of any professional environment. They serve as a framework for planning and executing tasks, providing a sense of urgency and accountability. However, in the pursuit of meeting deadlines, individuals often face the challenge of setting unrealistic timeframes, leading to stress, subpar work, or missed targets.

When setting a deadline, it is crucial to assess the scope and complexity of the task at hand. A thorough understanding of the various components involved enables a more accurate estimation of the time required for completion. This involves breaking down the project into smaller, manageable segments, each with its own timeline. It's important to account for potential obstacles or unforeseen circumstances that may arise during the process, allowing for a buffer in the schedule to mitigate any delays. By applying this methodical approach, individuals can set pragmatic deadlines that align with the task's requirements.

To ensure the adherence to the established timelines, it is imperative to leverage task management tools and methodologies.

Utilizing project management software, creating *Gantt charts*, or employing agile frameworks can aid in visualizing the workflow, identifying dependencies, and maintaining an overview of the project timeline. Periodic reassessment of the deadlines and flexibility to make necessary adjustments based on the evolving circumstances are crucial for sustaining alignment with the project objectives.

Meeting deadlines is not merely about completing tasks on time; it encompasses delivering quality outcomes within the stipulated timeframe. This necessitates striking a balance between efficiency and excellence, avoiding the temptation to compromise on the standard of work to meet deadlines. Practicing effective time management techniques, prioritizing tasks, and delegating responsibilities optimally contribute to optimizing productivity without compromising on quality.

Promoting a culture of recognizing and celebrating timely achievements instills a spirit of accomplishment and motivation among the team. In conclusion, mastering the art of setting realistic deadlines and consistently meeting them involves a holistic approach encompassing meticulous planning, transparent communication, strategic utilization of tools, and a commitment to delivering quality results. By cultivating a mindset centered around accountability, adaptability, and continuous improvement, individuals and organizations can navigate through challenges, uphold their commitments, and achieve sustained success.

Mastering the Art of Saying No

Setting boundaries and managing one's time effectively often requires the ability to decline requests or opportunities that do not align with your priorities. *Learning to say 'no' is not about being negative or unhelpful – rather, it is about protecting your time and energy for the things that matter most.* Saying 'no' respectfully and assertively can prevent overcommitment and burnout while allowing you to focus on activities that contribute to your goals.

It's important to communicate your 'no' effectively. Clearly articulating your reasons for declining a request can help the other party understand your perspective and minimize potential misunderstandings. By expressing appreciation for the opportunity and diplomatically explaining your current workload or conflicting priorities, you can maintain positive relationships while setting realistic expectations.

Another aspect of mastering the art of saying 'no' is understanding the difference between genuine opportunities for growth and distractions that hinder progress. Evaluating each request against your values and objectives enables you to make informed decisions about where to invest your time and efforts. It empowers you to discern between beneficial endeavors and endeavors that may detract from your long-term success.

Developing alternative solutions when declining a request can demonstrate your willingness to support others while prioritizing your commitments. This could involve suggesting an alternative resource, recommending another colleague, or proposing a different approach that aligns with your capacity. It showcases your proactive and collaborative mindset, reinforcing your dedication to mutual success.

Mastering the art of saying 'no' requires self-awareness, confidence, and a strategic mindset. It involves recognizing that prioritizing your well-being and goals is not selfish but necessary for sustained productivity and fulfillment. By cultivating this skill, you can cultivate a more intentional and purposeful professional and personal journey.

Technology for Smarter Workflows

Today, the use of technology has become integral to optimizing productivity and streamlining workflows. Leveraging the right technology can revolutionize the way we work, providing us with tools that not only save time but also enhance the quality of our outputs.

From project management software to communication platforms, there is a wide array of technological solutions available to help professionals work smarter. Adopting these tools allows individuals and teams to collaborate more efficiently, track progress, and stay organized amidst the demands of modern work environments. Task management apps provide real-time visibility into ongoing projects, enabling better delegation and deadline management. This results in enhanced accountability and improved task prioritization.

Incorporating cloud-based storage solutions ensures seamless access to essential documents and data from any location, promoting flexibility and remote work capabilities. Automation tools further simplify repetitive tasks, freeing up valuable time for more critical and creative endeavors. By harnessing technology's power, professionals can create custom workflows tailored to their unique needs, optimizing efficiency and minimizing unnecessary manual effort. Embracing technology also contributes to sustainable work practices by reducing paper usage and minimizing environmental impact. However, it is crucial to remain mindful of the potential drawbacks, such as information security risks and overreliance on automation. Striking a balance between leveraging technology for its advantages while mitigating its potential downsides is essential.

Mastering the art of integrating technology into workflows empowers individuals to achieve optimal productivity, successfully navigate challenges, and deliver exceptional results.

Balancing Professional and Personal Life

Achieving a harmonious balance between professional and personal life is a perpetual challenge in the modern world. This pivotal aspect of time management directly influences overall well-being, productivity, and satisfaction. The quest for equilibrium requires introspection, strategic planning, and a commitment to setting boundaries that respect the individual's mental, physical, and emotional needs. *Understanding the value of downtime and leisure as essential components of a healthy lifestyle is the cornerstone of this delicate balance. It involves recognizing that one's personal life is not secondary but complementary to their professional endeavors.* Cultivating a supportive network of family and friends, along with engaging in enriching hobbies or activities, can provide fulfillment beyond the confines of the workplace.

Establishing clear-cut priorities and adhering to them is paramount. Effective time allocation ensures that both personal and professional commitments are adequately addressed. This entails delineating specific periods for work-related tasks and allocating ample time for personal pursuits, thereby preventing burnout and fostering sustained motivation. Identifying and mitigating potential sources of stress within both spheres is crucial. By openly communicating expectations, concerns, and limitations with colleagues and loved ones, individuals can cultivate an environment that fosters understanding and facilitates mutual support.

Utilizing technology as a means to streamline work processes and enhance communication, particularly when working remotely, allows for increased flexibility and can contribute to achieving a healthier balance. Recognizing that each person's concept of balance is subjective is integral; therefore, it is imperative to tailor strategies to suit individual needs and circumstances. Embracing adaptability and mindfulness empowers individuals to recalibrate their approach as life's demands evolve, cultivating resilience and an enduring sense of equilibrium. Striking a harmonious balance between professional aspirations and personal fulfilment epitomizes the essence of effective time management, encompassing the holistic well-being and fulfillment crucial for leading a purposeful life.

Achieving a healthy work-life balance is essential for long-term productivity and well-being. By managing your time effectively and setting boundaries, you can maintain a balance between professional and personal life. The strategies for achieving and maintaining work-life balance include but not limited to the following

1. Setting Boundaries:

Defining Work Hours: Establish clear work hours and stick to them. Communicate your availability to colleagues and clients to manage expectations.

Personal Time Protection: Protect your personal time by avoiding work-related tasks outside of designated work hours. Use this time to relax, recharge, and pursue personal interests.

2. Prioritizing Self-Care:

Physical Health: Incorporate regular exercise, a healthy diet, and sufficient sleep into your routine. Physical well-being is crucial for maintaining energy and focus.

Mental Health: Practice mindfulness, meditation, or other stress-relief techniques. Taking care of your mental health helps you stay resilient and productive.

3. Effective Time Management at Home:

Planning Personal Activities: Plan and schedule personal activities just as you would with work tasks. This ensures you make time for family, hobbies, and relaxation.

Sharing Responsibilities: Share household responsibilities with family members or roommates. Collaboration at home reduces stress and frees up time for personal enjoyment.

4. Flexibility and Adaptability:

Adapting to Change: Be flexible in adjusting your work-life balance as needed. Life circumstances and work demands can change, requiring you to adapt your approach.

Remote Work Strategies: If working remotely, establish a dedicated workspace and set boundaries to separate work from personal life. Maintain regular routines to balance both aspects effectively.

5. Reflecting and Adjusting:

Regular Reflection: Reflect on your work-life balance regularly. Identify areas for improvement and make necessary adjustments to maintain a healthy equilibrium.

Seeking Support: Reach out to mentors, colleagues, or professional coaches for advice on managing work-life balance. Support from others can provide valuable insights and encouragement.

Strategies for Self-Improvement

Effective time management is essential for leadership excellence. Here are the top time management challenges leaders face and strategies for becoming a problem solver through self-development and improvement:

Prioritizing Tasks

Challenge: Determining which tasks are most important and urgent, especially when everything seems critical.

Self-Development Strategies:

Prioritization Techniques:

- *Eisenhower Matrix:* Use the Eisenhower Matrix to categorize tasks into four quadrants: urgent and important, important but not urgent, urgent but not important, and neither urgent nor important. Focus on the first two quadrants.

- *ABC Method*: Rank tasks by priority (A for highest priority, B for medium, and C for low). Tackle 'A' tasks first.

Goal Setting:

- *SMART Goals*: Set SMART goals (Specific, Measurable, Achievable, Relevant, Time-bound) to clarify priorities and focus on tasks that align with your objectives.

- *Daily and Weekly Planning*: Plan your days and weeks in advance, allocating time to high-priority tasks first.

Reflect and Adjust:

- *Review:* Regularly review your task list and adjust priorities based on changing circumstances and new information.
- *Feedback Loop*: Seek feedback from colleagues and mentors on your prioritization and adjust accordingly.

2. Avoiding Procrastination

Challenge: Delaying important tasks in favor of less critical, easier tasks.

Self-Development Strategies:

Understanding Procrastination:

- *Self-Awareness*: Reflect on why you procrastinate. Common reasons include fear of failure, perfectionism, and feeling overwhelmed.
- *Triggers:* Identify triggers that lead to procrastination and develop strategies to mitigate them.

Breaking Tasks into Smaller Steps:

- *Chunking:* Break large tasks into smaller, manageable steps. This makes tasks less intimidating and easier to start.

- *Microtasks:* Set microtasks with short deadlines to build momentum and maintain progress.

Accountability:

- *Accountability Partners:* Work with an accountability partner who can help keep you on track and motivated.

- *Commitment Devices*: Use commitment devices like setting deadlines and creating external consequences for not completing tasks.

3. Managing Interruptions and Distractions

Challenge: Staying focused in the face of constant interruptions and distractions, especially in a dynamic work environment.

Self-Development Strategies:

Creating a Focused Environment:

- *Workspace Setup:* Design your workspace to minimize distractions. This might include a quiet area, noise-canceling headphones, or a designated 'do not disturb' time.

- *Digital Distractions:* Use tools and apps that block distracting websites and notifications during focused work periods.

Time Blocking:

- *Scheduled Focus Time*: Allocate specific blocks of time for focused work, during which you avoid meetings, emails, and other interruptions.

- *Pomodoro Technique:* Use the Pomodoro Technique to work in focused intervals (e.g., 25 minutes of work followed by a 5-minute break).

Communication Management:

- *Set Boundaries:* Clearly communicate your availability and preferred communication times to colleagues.

- *Delegate:* Delegate tasks and responsibilities to team members to reduce the number of interruptions you need to handle personally.

4. Balancing Multiple Responsibilities

Challenge: Juggling various roles and responsibilities without compromising on performance in any area.

Self-Development Strategies:

Delegation:

- *Empower Team Members:* Delegate tasks to capable team members, allowing you to focus on higher-level responsibilities.

- *Trust and Verify*: Trust your team but also implement a system to verify progress and provide support as needed.

Time Management Tools:

- *Task Management* Apps: Use task management apps like Trello, Asana, or Microsoft To-Do to keep track of responsibilities and deadlines.

- *Calendars:* Maintain an up-to-date calendar to schedule and prioritize tasks and meetings effectively.

Routine and Habits:

- *Daily Routine*: Establish a daily routine that includes time for strategic planning, task execution, and breaks.

- *Healthy Habits:* Develop healthy habits like regular exercise, adequate sleep, and mindfulness practices *to maintain energy and focus.*

5. Setting and Maintaining Boundaries

Challenge: Establishing and maintaining boundaries between work and personal life to prevent burnout and maintain productivity.

Self-Development Strategies:

Work-Life Balance:

- *Clear Boundaries:* Set clear boundaries for work hours and personal time. Communicate these boundaries to your team and adhere to them.

- *Rest and Recovery:* Schedule regular breaks, vacations, and downtime to recharge and prevent burnout.

Mindfulness and Stress Management:

- *Mindfulness Practices*: Incorporate mindfulness practices like deep breathing exercises into your daily routine to manage stress and stay focused.

- *Stress Management* Techniques: Learn and apply stress management techniques to handle pressure effectively.

Reflective Practice:

- *Regular Reflection:* Set aside time for regular reflection on your time management practices. Identify what works, what doesn't, and make adjustments as needed.

- *Feedback:* Seek feedback from colleagues, mentors, and family members to ensure your boundaries are respected and effective.

5

FINANCIAL ACUMEN

"Financial acumen is the cornerstone of sustainable success. It involves not only understanding numbers but also interpreting their stories to make informed decisions that drive growth, mitigate risk, and ensure long-term prosperity."

Understanding Financial Principles

Financial acumen is crucial for making informed business decisions, managing resources effectively, and driving organizational success. A solid understanding of financial principles forms the foundation of this competency.

1. Basic Financial Statements:

Income Statement: Learn how to read and interpret income statements, which show a company's revenues, expenses, and profits over a specific period. Understand the significance of key components such as gross profit, operating income, and net income.

Balance Sheet: Understand the structure of a balance sheet, which provides a snapshot of a company's assets, liabilities, and shareholders' equity at a specific point in time. Familiarize yourself with terms like current assets, long-term liabilities, and equity.

Cash Flow Statement: Analyze cash flow statements to track the flow of cash into and out of a business. Understand the importance of operating, investing, and financing activities in maintaining liquidity.

2. Key Financial Ratios:

Profitability Ratios: Learn about profitability ratios such as gross margin, operating margin, and *return on equity (ROE)*. These ratios help assess a company's ability to generate profit relative to its revenue, assets, and equity.

Liquidity Ratios: Understand liquidity ratios like the current ratio and quick ratio, which measure a company's ability to meet short-term obligations. These ratios are crucial for evaluating financial stability.

Solvency Ratios: Familiarize yourself with solvency ratios such as the debt-to-equity ratio and interest coverage ratio. These ratios assess a company's long-term financial health and its ability to meet long-term obligations.

Efficiency Ratios: Study efficiency ratios like inventory turnover and accounts receivable turnover. These ratios provide insights into how effectively a company utilizes its assets.

3. Budgeting and Forecasting:

Creating Budgets: Learn how to create and manage budgets to allocate resources effectively. Understand the importance of setting financial goals, estimating revenues and expenses, and monitoring performance against the budget.

Financial Forecasting: Develop skills in financial forecasting to predict future financial performance. Use historical data, market trends, and economic indicators to make informed projections.

4. Cost Management:

Fixed and Variable Costs: Differentiate between fixed costs (unchanging with production volume) and variable costs (varying with production volume). Understanding these concepts helps in cost control and pricing decisions.

Break-Even Analysis: Conduct break-even analysis to determine the level of sales needed to cover costs. This analysis helps in setting sales targets and pricing strategies.

5. Investment and Capital Allocation:

Capital Budgeting: Learn about capital budgeting techniques such as *Net Present Value (NPV), Internal Rate of Return (IRR), and Payback Period.* These methods help evaluate the profitability of long-term investments.

Cost of Capital: Understand the concept of the cost of capital and its components, including the cost of debt and equity. Knowing the cost of capital is essential for making investment decisions.

6. Financial Decision-Making:

Risk Assessment: Assess financial risks and incorporate risk management strategies into decision-making processes. Understand the impact of financial leverage, market fluctuations, and economic conditions on business operations.

Return on Investment (ROI): Calculate ROI to evaluate the efficiency of investments. A high ROI indicates that the investment gains compare favorably to its cost.

7. Taxation and Compliance:

Tax Regulations: Familiarize yourself with relevant tax regulations and their implications for business operations. Understanding tax obligations helps in compliance and financial planning.

Financial Compliance: Ensure adherence to financial regulations and standards, such as Generally Accepted Accounting Principles (GAAP) or International Financial Reporting Standards (IFRS).

8. Financial Planning:

Strategic Financial Planning: Integrate financial planning into overall business strategy. Align financial goals with business objectives to ensure long-term sustainability.

Personal Financial Planning: Develop personal financial literacy to manage personal finances effectively. Understanding personal finance principles can also enhance overall financial acumen.

9. Tools and Technology:

Financial Software: Utilize financial software and tools to streamline financial management processes. Familiarize yourself with accounting software, financial modeling tools, and data analytics platforms.

Data Analysis: Leverage data analytics to gain insights into financial performance. Use data visualization tools to present financial data clearly and effectively.

10. Continuous Learning:

Professional Development: Engage in continuous learning to stay updated on financial principles and industry trends. Attend workshops, pursue certifications, and participate in professional organizations.

Staying Informed: Keep abreast of economic news, market developments, and regulatory changes. Staying informed enhances your ability to make informed financial decisions.

Understanding financial principles is fundamental for effective financial management and strategic decision-making. By mastering these concepts, you can enhance your financial acumen and contribute to the success of your organization.

Budgeting Basics

Budgeting is a fundamental aspect of financial management that plays a crucial role in the success of individuals and organizations alike. It involves the process of creating a comprehensive plan that outlines the expected income and expenses over a specific period. By effectively managing finances through budgeting, individuals and businesses can make informed decisions, allocate resources efficiently, and achieve their financial goals. A well-structured budget not only provides a clear roadmap for financial operations but also serves as a tool for monitoring and controlling expenditures.

To begin with, the first step in establishing an effective budget is to gather all relevant financial data, including income sources, fixed and variable expenses, investments, and savings. This comprehensive understanding of the financial landscape forms the foundation for developing a realistic and achievable budget. Once the financial information is compiled, it is essential to categorize the expenses into essential and non-essential items. This categorization helps prioritize spending and ensures that critical financial obligations are met before discretionary expenses.

Budgeting involves setting measurable financial goals and aligning the allocation of resources with these objectives. Whether it's saving for a major purchase, reducing debt, or planning for retirement, a well-defined budget facilitates the process of realizing these aspirations. Additionally, budgeting enables individuals and organizations to adapt to changing financial circumstances and anticipate potential challenges, ultimately enhancing their financial resilience.

Using technological advancements in budgeting tools and applications can streamline the budgeting process, improve accuracy, and provide real-time insights into financial performance. These tools offer features such as expense tracking, automated bill payments, and customized financial reports, empowering users to make data-driven decisions. Utilizing such technologies allows for greater efficiency and precision in managing budgets, ensuring optimal utilization of financial resources.

Mastering budgeting basics is paramount for achieving long-term financial stability and prosperity. By cultivating a disciplined approach to budgeting and integrating modern financial tools, individuals and businesses can gain greater control over their finances, mitigate unnecessary risks, and strategically allocate resources for sustainable growth and success.

Investment Principles

To master the art of investment, one must develop a deep understanding of investment principles. Successful investing requires knowledge, strategy, and discipline. *At its core, investment is about making choices today that will positively impact your financial future.* Investment principles encompass a wide range of concepts, from risk management to diversification. When considering investments, it's crucial to assess the potential returns against the level of risk. *Diversification, the practice of spreading investments across different asset classes and sectors, is a key principle in managing risk.*

Having a clear investment strategy and sticking to a long-term plan can help navigate market volatility and capitalize on opportunities. Another important principle is *conducting thorough research and due diligence before committing to any investment.* This involves analyzing historical performance, evaluating market trends, and understanding the fundamental aspects of the investment.

Understanding the concept of compounding returns is essential for long-term success. By reinvesting earnings, one can accelerate wealth accumulation over time. It's also vital to align investment decisions with personal financial goals and risk tolerance. Doing so ensures that every investment fits within an overarching financial strategy. Staying informed about economic indicators, geopolitical events, and industry developments is critical for making informed investment decisions. Ethical considerations in investing cannot be overlooked. Sustainable and responsible investing practices are increasingly important in today's global landscape. Adhering to ethical investment principles not only aligns with values but can also contribute to long-term stability and growth. Mastering these investment principles lays the foundation for sound decision-making and successful wealth management.

Risk Management

Risk management is a crucial aspect of financial acumen, particularly in the context of investment and business operations. It involves identifying, assessing, and mitigating potential risks that could adversely impact the financial stability and performance of an organization. *Effective risk management entails a thorough understanding of various types of risks, including market risk, credit risk, operational risk, and liquidity risk.* Market risk refers to the potential for financial losses due to fluctuations in market prices, interest rates, or exchange rates. Credit risk involves the possibility of counterparties failing to meet their financial obligations, leading to losses for the organization. Operational risk encompasses the potential for disruptions or losses arising from internal processes, people, systems, or external events. Liquidity risk pertains to the ability of an organization to meet its short-term financial obligations. To manage these risks effectively, organizations employ a range of strategies and tools. These may include diversification of investments, setting up risk management committees, utilizing financial derivatives for hedging, implementing robust internal controls, and maintaining adequate levels of liquidity.

Risk management also involves creating contingency plans and stress testing various scenarios to assess the impact of adverse events on the financial health of the organization. By proactively addressing potential risks, organizations can enhance their resilience and adaptability in the face of uncertainties, ultimately safeguarding their financial well-being. In today's dynamic and interconnected global business environment, the ability to navigate and mitigate risks is a critical skill for any individual or organization seeking long-term financial success.

Cost Control Strategies

Successful businesses understand the critical importance of effective cost control. Cost control strategies are essential for managing and optimizing a company's financial resources to achieve sustainable growth and long-term success. In today's competitive business environment, organizations constantly face challenges related to rising operational costs, fluctuating market conditions, and evolving consumer demands. Consequently, implementing and maintaining robust cost control strategies is vital to ensure profitability and maintain a competitive edge.

One of the fundamental aspects of cost control is the identification and analysis of all expenses incurred in the operation of a business. This involves categorizing expenses into fixed and variable costs, analyzing cost patterns, and identifying opportunities for cost reduction. By leveraging this data, businesses can develop targeted cost control strategies that align with their organizational goals and objectives.

Effective cost control requires a proactive approach to monitoring and managing expenses. Businesses should regularly assess their cost structures, identify areas of inefficiency, and implement measures to eliminate wasteful spending. This can involve renegotiating contracts with suppliers, streamlining internal processes, and embracing technology solutions that automate routine tasks and reduce overhead expenses.

In addition to reducing costs, businesses must also focus on enhancing the value derived from their expenditures. This entails evaluating the quality and necessity of each expense to ensure that it contributes to the overall productivity and profitability of the organization. By prioritizing investments that yield significant returns and eliminating non-essential expenses, businesses can strategically allocate resources to drive growth and innovation.

The culture of cost consciousness among employees is pivotal in successful cost control management. Engaging and educating employees on the significance of cost control, involving them in decision-making processes, and incentivizing resourcefulness can lead to collective efforts in driving cost savings across the organization.

Effective cost control strategies are not solely about cutting expenses; *they are about optimizing the allocation of resources to support sustainable business growth while ensuring financial stability.* By consistently evaluating, refining, and adapting cost control measures, businesses can mitigate financial risks, improve operational efficiency, and position themselves for long-term success in the dynamic marketplace.

Economic Indicators

Economic indicators are essential tools for understanding the overall health and performance of an economy. These indicators provide valuable insights into various aspects such as employment, production, consumer spending, business profits, and overall economic activity. By analyzing these indicators, businesses, policymakers, and investors can make informed decisions to navigate through economic trends and challenges.

One of the key economic indicators is the *Gross Domestic Product (GDP)*, which measures the total value of goods and services produced within a country. GDP growth or contraction provides vital information about the economy's expansion or potential recession. Another one is the *Consumer Price Index (CPI) reflects changes in the cost of living and inflation rates, impacting consumer purchasing power and investment strategies.*

Unemployment rate is another crucial economic indicator that measures the percentage of the total workforce that is unemployed and actively seeking employment. *This indicator offers insight into the labor market's strength and can influence government policies and business strategies.* The *Purchasing Managers' Index (PMI)* provides data on manufacturing and service sector activities, offering early signals of economic trends and potential shifts.

Other significant indicators include housing data, including new and existing home sales, construction permits, and housing starts, providing insights into the real estate market's strength. The retail sales report reflects consumer spending patterns, providing indications of overall economic health and consumer confidence.

Understanding and analyzing these economic indicators is crucial for businesses to anticipate market trends, assess risk, and make strategic decisions. By staying abreast of these metrics, organizations can adapt their business strategies, manage financial resources effectively, and identify growth opportunities amidst dynamic economic conditions.

Financial Forecasting Techniques

The ability to accurately forecast financial outcomes is crucial for the success of any business. Financial forecasting techniques provide valuable insights that help organizations make strategic decisions and plan for the future. In this section, we will explore various methods and approaches used in financial forecasting. One common technique is the use of historical data to identify patterns and trends that can be projected into the future. This approach relies on past performance as an indicator of future results, allowing businesses to anticipate potential opportunities and challenges. Another important method is scenario analysis, which involves creating multiple financial models based on different possible scenarios. By assessing the potential impacts of various scenarios, organizations can better prepare for uncertainties and mitigate risks. *Regression analysis is a powerful tool for identifying relationships between different variables and predicting financial outcomes.* By analyzing historical data and establishing correlations, businesses can make informed forecasts and evaluate the impact of various factors.

Time series analysis involves examining data points collected at regular intervals to identify patterns and make predictions. This method is particularly useful for understanding seasonal fluctuations and cyclical trends in financial data. Moving beyond traditional statistical methods, the use of advanced technologies such as artificial intelligence and machine learning has revolutionized financial forecasting.

These technologies enable businesses to analyze vast amounts of data and derive complex insights, improving the accuracy and reliability of forecasts. When implementing financial forecasting techniques, it is essential to consider the limitations and risks associated with each method. While historical data provides valuable insight, it may not always reflect future market conditions or unexpected events. Scenario analyses require meticulous attention to detail and consideration of various external factors that could influence outcomes. Similarly, regression and time series analyses rely on the assumption of consistent patterns, which may not hold true in volatile or unpredictable environments. Lastly, leveraging advanced technologies demands a robust understanding of data analytics and the ability to interpret complex algorithms effectively.

Therefore, it is imperative for organizations to combine these techniques with expert judgment and market knowledge to enhance the accuracy of financial forecasts. Mastering financial forecasting techniques empowers businesses to make informed decisions, anticipate market trends, and navigate uncertainties with confidence. Through a comprehensive understanding of these methods and their applications, organizations can optimize their financial strategies and drive sustainable growth.

Leveraging Financial Technology

Leveraging financial technology encompasses a broad spectrum of tools and platforms designed to streamline various financial processes, enhance decision-making, and optimize resource allocation. From advanced analytics and machine learning algorithms to blockchain and cloud-based solutions, the realm of financial technology offers boundless opportunities for businesses to revolutionize their operations. By harnessing the power of automation and real-time data analysis, organizations can gain valuable insights into market trends, customer behaviors, and risk factors, enabling them to make informed and proactive financial decisions. *The adoption of digital payment systems and mobile banking applications not only enhances convenience for customers but also facilitates seamless transaction processing and fund management.*

The significance of cybersecurity in the realm of financial technology cannot be overstated, as the prevalence of digital transactions necessitates robust measures to safeguard sensitive financial information. With cyber threats becoming increasingly sophisticated, the implementation of encryption protocols, multi-factor authentication, and stringent access controls is imperative to mitigate potential security breaches.

The emergence of fintech startups and disruptors has ushered in a new era of innovation, challenging traditional financial institutions to embrace agile technologies and adapt to changing market dynamics. Collaboration with fintech firms presents opportunities for incumbents to leverage cutting-edge solutions in areas such as peer-to-peer lending, robo-advisory services, and digital currency exchanges. As the financial technology ecosystem continues to evolve, it is essential for professionals to stay abreast of the latest developments and acquire digital literacy to capitalize on the transformative potential of these innovations. By cultivating a culture of technological agility and embracing continuous learning, organizations can effectively leverage financial technology to drive sustainable growth and remain at the forefront of the ever-changing financial landscape.

Ethics in Financial Decision-Making

Ethics in financial decision-making is a crucial aspect of maintaining trust and credibility in the business world. As companies strive for profitability and growth, ethical considerations often take a backseat, but their importance cannot be overstated. In today's complex and interconnected global economy, ethical lapses can have far-reaching consequences, affecting not only the involved individuals and organizations but also the larger community and environment. Therefore, it is imperative for professionals to navigate the intricate web of financial decisions with integrity and moral responsibility.

Ethical dilemmas in finance often arise when individuals or corporations face conflicting interests. When making investment decisions or engaging in financial transactions, there may be temptations to prioritize short-term gains over long-term sustainability, or to bend the rules to achieve immediate competitive advantage. However, succumbing to these temptations can lead to severe repercussions, damaging reputations and eroding stakeholder trust. It is essential for financial professionals to resist these pressures and adhere to a code of ethical conduct that promotes transparency, fairness, and accountability.

One fundamental principle of ethical financial decision-making is *honesty*. Honest and transparent communication about financial matters creates an environment of trust and reliability, both internally and externally. Misleading or concealing information can lead to misunderstanding and misinterpretation, ultimately leading to damaging consequences. Ethical decision-making involves considering the impact of financial choices on various stakeholders, including employees, customers, investors, and the broader community. It requires weighing the financial benefits against potential social and environmental costs, striving for sustainable and responsible outcomes.

Another critical aspect of ethical financial decision-making is *compliance with legal and regulatory frameworks*. This involves not only understanding and following existing laws and regulations but also actively participating in shaping and promoting ethical standards within the industry. By adhering to ethical guidelines and advocating for fair and just financial practices, professionals can contribute to the overall integrity and stability of the financial system. Promoting a culture of ethical decision-making within organizations can mitigate the risk of non-compliance and unethical behavior, safeguarding the reputation and sustainability of the business.

Ethics in financial decision-making should be regarded as a cornerstone of professional conduct in the financial sector. Upholding ethical standards in financial practices is essential for preserving trust, credibility, and the long-term viability of organizations. By prioritizing integrity, honesty, accountability, and compliance, financial professionals can navigate the complexities of the modern financial landscape while contributing to a more ethical and sustainable global economy.

Strategies for Self-Improvement

Financial acumen is a crucial skill for leaders, involving the ability to understand and manage financial resources effectively. Here are challenges and strategies for overcoming them:

1. Understanding Financial Statements

Challenge: Interpreting financial statements such as balance sheets, income statements, and cash flow statements can be complex, especially for leaders without a background in finance.

Self-Development Strategies:

Financial Education:

- *Courses and Workshops:* Enroll in finance courses or workshops that cover the basics of financial statements. Look for programs offered by universities, business schools, or online platforms like Coursera and Udemy.

- *Certifications:* Consider pursuing certifications such as CFA (Chartered Financial Analyst) or CPA (Certified Public Accountant) to deepen your understanding.

Practical Application:

- *Case Studies:* Study financial case studies to see real-world applications of financial statement analysis.
- *Hands-On Practice*: Analyze your organization's financial statements or those of publicly traded companies to practice your skills.

Mentorship:

- *Finance Mentors*: Seek mentorship from finance professionals within your organization or industry. Learn from their experience and ask for guidance on interpreting financial data.
- *Peer Learning:* Join finance-focused study groups or discussion forums to share knowledge and learn from peers.

2. Budgeting and Forecasting

Challenge: Creating accurate budgets and forecasts that align with organizational goals and adapt to changing conditions.

Self-Development Strategies:

Budgeting Skills:

- *Workshops and Seminars:* Attend workshops and seminars on budgeting techniques and best practices.

- *Software Training:* Learn to use budgeting and forecasting software like Excel, QuickBooks, or specialized tools like Adaptive Insights.

Forecasting Techniques:

- *Statistical Methods:* Study statistical methods and tools used in forecasting. Courses in statistics and econometrics can be beneficial.

- *Scenario Analysis:* Practice scenario analysis to understand how different variables impact your forecasts and budget plans.

Continuous Improvement:

- *Regular Reviews:* Regularly review and adjust your budgets and forecasts based on actual performance and market changes.

- *Feedback*: Seek feedback from colleagues and financial advisors to refine your budgeting and forecasting processes.

3. Cost Management and Optimization

Challenge: Identifying and managing costs effectively to improve profitability without compromising quality or efficiency.

Self-Development Strategies:

Cost Analysis:

- *Lean Principles:* Study lean management principles and practices to identify waste and optimize processes.

- *Cost Accounting:* Learn about cost accounting methods to better track and control costs within your organization.

Process Improvement:

- *Continuous Improvement:* Implement continuous improvement methodologies like Six Sigma to streamline operations and reduce costs.

- *Benchmarking:* Compare your organization's costs and processes against industry benchmarks to identify areas for improvement.

Strategic Cost Management:

- *Cost-Benefit Analysis:* Practice conducting cost-benefit analyses to make informed decisions about expenditures and investments.

- *Efficiency Programs:* Develop and lead efficiency programs within your organization to foster a culture of cost consciousness and optimization.

4. Investment Decisions

Challenge: Making informed investment decisions that align with the organization's strategic goals and risk tolerance.

Self-Development Strategies:

Investment Analysis:

- *Financial Models:* Learn to build and interpret financial models used in investment analysis, such as discounted cash flow (DCF) and net present value (NPV).

- *Risk Assessment:* Study risk assessment techniques to evaluate potential investments' risks and returns.

Market Knowledge:

- *Market Research:* Stay informed about market trends, economic indicators, and industry developments that impact investment decisions.

- *Investment Courses:* Take courses on investment management and financial markets to deepen your understanding of various investment vehicles and strategies.

Strategic Alignment:

- *Investment Policy:* Develop a clear investment policy that aligns with your organization's strategic goals and risk appetite.

- *Review and Adjust*: Regularly review your investment portfolio and adjust based on performance and changing market conditions.

5. Financial Risk Management

Challenge: Identifying, assessing, and mitigating financial risks to protect the organization's assets and ensure long-term stability.

Self-Development Strategies:

Risk Management Frameworks:

- *ERM:* Study enterprise risk management (ERM) frameworks to understand how to systematically identify and manage risks across the organization.
- *Certification*: Consider certifications such as FRM (Financial Risk Manager) to enhance your risk management skills.

Risk Assessment Tools:

- *Quantitative Methods*: Learn quantitative methods for risk assessment, including Value at Risk (VaR) and stress testing.

- *Scenario Planning:* Use scenario planning and simulation techniques to anticipate and prepare for potential financial risks.

Risk Mitigation Strategies:

- *Hedging:* Study hedging strategies to protect against financial risks such as currency fluctuations and interest rate changes.

- *Diversification*: Learn about diversification techniques to spread risk across different investments and asset classes.

6

PROJECT MANAGEMENT

"Project management is the disciplined art of turning vision into reality. By harmonizing resources, timelines, and objectives, we navigate complexity and drive progress, transforming ambitious goals into achieved milestones."

What is it?

Project management is the discipline of planning, organizing, and managing resources to bring about the successful completion of specific project goals and objectives. In today's dynamic business environment, project management plays a crucial role in achieving organizational success. It provides the framework for effectively addressing challenges, mitigating risks, and delivering value to stakeholders. With the increasing complexity of modern projects, businesses are recognizing the significance of project management as a key driver of competitiveness and operational excellence. By adopting robust project management practices, organizations can enhance their ability to adapt to change, optimize resource allocation, and achieve strategic alignment.

Project management enables businesses to streamline operations, improve productivity, and maintain a competitive edge in the market. As the cornerstone of efficient project delivery, project management is instrumental in driving innovation, harnessing collaboration, and ensuring the timely and cost-effective execution of initiatives. Embracing project management principles empowers businesses to navigate uncertainties, capitalize on opportunities, and achieve sustainable growth. In essence, project management is not only a methodology but also a mindset that fosters accountability, transparency, and continuous improvement across all levels of an organization.

Understanding Project Life Cycles

Projects, regardless of their nature or scale, go through distinct phases known as project life cycles. Understanding these life cycles is crucial for effective project management and successful completion. *The project life cycle typically consists of initiation, planning, execution, monitoring and controlling, and closing phases.* Each phase serves a unique purpose and requires specific approaches and tools.

The *initiation phase* marks the beginning of a project, where the need for the project is identified, and its feasibility is assessed. This involves defining a clear project scope, identifying stakeholders, and conducting initial risk assessments. Once the project is approved, the *planning phase* begins, during which detailed plans and strategies are developed. This phase includes creating project schedules, allocating resources, and establishing key performance indicators to measure progress.

As the project moves into the *execution phase*, the work outlined in the project plan is carried out. Effective leadership and team coordination play a critical role in this phase to ensure tasks are completed as per the outlined plan. Simultaneously, the *monitoring and controlling phase* involves continuous assessment of project performance against the predefined objectives. This phase requires regular reporting, risk management, and making necessary adjustments to keep the project on track.

Lastly, the *closing phase* involves formally completing the project, obtaining client acceptance, and ensuring all deliverables are met. A comprehensive review is conducted to identify lessons learned and best practices for future projects. It also involves transitioning the project output to the operational team if applicable.

Understanding the project life cycle provides a roadmap for project managers to navigate through different stages effectively. *It informs decision-making, resource allocation, risk management, and communication strategies unique to each phase.* By comprehensively understanding project life cycles, project managers can streamline processes, anticipate challenges, and ultimately lead their teams to successful project completion.

Effective Planning

Effective planning is the cornerstone of successful project management. It involves a structured approach to defining the scope, objectives, and deliverables of a project, as well as outlining the tasks, resources, and timelines required to achieve these goals. In this section, we will explore various tools and techniques that can be utilized to enhance the planning phase of any project.

1. *Work Breakdown Structure (WBS)*: This technique involves breaking down the project scope into smaller, more manageable components. By organizing the work into hierarchical levels, the WBS helps in visualizing the entire scope and ensures that no important task is overlooked during planning.
2. *Gantt Charts*: Gantt charts are powerful visual tools that display the project schedule, depicting the start and finish dates of individual tasks. They help in identifying dependencies, tracking progress, and managing resource allocation effectively.
3. *Critical Path Method (CPM):* CPM is a method used to identify the longest sequence of dependent activities that determines the shortest possible duration for completing the project. By identifying the critical path, project managers can focus on the most time-sensitive tasks and optimize the overall schedule.
4. *Resource Leveling*: This technique involves adjusting the project schedule to ensure that available resources are utilized efficiently without overloading or

underutilizing them. By smoothing out resource allocations, it helps in minimizing project delays and maintaining a balanced workload across the team.
5. *Risk Analysis and Management:* Anticipating and managing risks is crucial for effective planning. Risk analysis techniques such as qualitative and quantitative risk assessments, risk registers, and contingency planning help in identifying potential threats and developing mitigation strategies to minimize their impact.
6. *Estimation Techniques*: Accurately estimating project costs, time, and resources is essential for effective planning. Various estimation techniques such as analogous estimating, parametric estimating, and three-point estimating aid in forecasting realistic project schedules and budgets.

By leveraging these tools and techniques for effective planning, project managers can improve their ability to anticipate and mitigate potential issues, optimize resource utilization, and maintain control over the project schedule and budget, ultimately leading to successful project outcomes.

Risk Management Strategies

Successful project management involves not only efficient planning and resource allocation, but also effective risk management strategies. In the realm of project management, risks are inherent and can manifest in various forms including scope creep, budget overruns, resource unavailability, market fluctuations, and unforeseen events. To mitigate these risks, it is crucial for project managers to adopt proactive risk management strategies that anticipate potential challenges and devise appropriate responses. There are several key steps involved in effective risk management.

The first step is *risk identification*, where project teams identify and assess potential risks that could impact the project's objectives. This involves conducting thorough risk assessments and collaborating with stakeholders to gain comprehensive insights. Once risks are identified, the next step is risk analysis, where the potential impact and likelihood of each risk are evaluated. This analysis helps prioritize risks based on their potential severity, allowing project teams to focus on addressing the most critical threats. Subsequently, risk mitigation strategies are developed to minimize the impact of identified risks. These strategies may include contingency planning, risk transfer through insurance, or risk avoidance by altering project plans. It is imperative to continuously monitor and review the effectiveness of risk mitigation strategies throughout the project lifecycle to adapt to evolving circumstances.

Maintaining clear communication channels among team members and stakeholders is vital for effective risk management. Regular risk reporting and updates ensure that all relevant parties are informed about potential threats and the status of mitigation efforts. Embracing a culture of transparency and accountability within the project team facilitates early detection and prompt response to emerging risks. *Another crucial aspect of risk management is being prepared to capitalize on potential opportunities that may arise amidst inherent project risks.* By actively seeking out and harnessing positive risks, project managers can create strategic advantages and innovation within the project. Integrating robust risk management strategies into project frameworks enhances the ability to deliver successful outcomes in the face of uncertainty and adversity.

Budgeting and Cost Control

Effective budgeting and cost control are critical components of successful project management. By carefully planning and managing financial resources, project managers can ensure that their projects stay on track and deliver value to stakeholders. Budgeting involves the process of estimating costs for various project activities, while cost control focuses on monitoring and managing these costs throughout the project lifecycle.

The first step in *budgeting* is to identify all potential costs associated with the project, including labor, materials, equipment, overhead, and any other relevant expenses. Project managers must then allocate funds to each activity based on these estimates, taking into account any potential risks or uncertainties that could impact costs. It's essential to create a realistic budget that aligns with the project scope and objectives while allowing for some flexibility to accommodate unforeseen changes.

Cost control involves actively monitoring expenses and ensuring that they remain within the planned budget. This requires diligent tracking of actual costs against the budgeted amounts, identifying any discrepancies or variances, and taking corrective action when necessary. Project managers may need to implement strategies to mitigate cost overruns, such as re-evaluating resource allocation, negotiating with vendors, or revising project timelines to optimize resource utilization.

Effective cost control also involves evaluating the *financial impact of any proposed changes or deviations from the original plan*. Project managers should carefully assess the potential cost implications of scope changes, additional requirements, or unexpected challenges, weighing the benefits against the associated costs before making decisions. This disciplined approach helps maintain financial discipline and protect the project's overall profitability and success.

In addition to managing direct project costs, project managers must also consider indirect costs and overhead expenses that can impact the project's financial performance. Understanding the full financial landscape of the project enables better decision-making and resource allocation, ensuring that all costs are accounted for and managed effectively.

Overall, budgeting and cost control are integral to project management, enabling project teams to operate within set financial parameters while delivering high-quality outcomes. With vigilant oversight and proactive management of project finances, organizations can achieve their project objectives while maximizing return on investment.

Team Dynamics and Leadership

Effective team dynamics and leadership are crucial for the successful execution of any project. In today's collaborative work environment, *understanding the intricacies of team dynamics and demonstrating strong leadership skills is paramount.* A project manager must be able to create a positive and productive team culture while also providing guidance and direction to ensure that the project goals are met.

One of the key aspects of team dynamics is understanding the strengths and weaknesses of each team member. By recognizing the unique abilities and talents within the team, a project manager can strategically delegate tasks and responsibilities, maximizing productivity and overall performance. Additionally, creating a supportive and inclusive environment where team members feel valued and respected can significantly enhance collaboration and innovation within the team.

Effective leadership is essential for motivating and inspiring team members to perform at their best. A project manager should possess strong communication skills, being able to clearly articulate the project vision, goals, and expectations. Moreover, a leader must be able to provide constructive feedback and support to team members, fostering continuous improvement and professional development.

A strong leader should be adept at conflict resolution and problem-solving, ensuring that any issues or disagreements within the team are addressed promptly and professionally. Building trust and rapport among team members is vital for maintaining a cohesive and high-performing team.

In today's global and diverse workforce, a project manager must also be cognizant of cultural differences and work style preferences within the team. Embracing diversity and inclusivity can lead to richer perspectives and creative solutions, ultimately leading to greater project success.

Ultimately, effective team dynamics and leadership are pivotal for driving project success. By prioritizing teamwork, nurturing a positive team environment, and demonstrating exemplary leadership, a project manager can empower their team to achieve remarkable results.

Quality Assurance in Projects

Ensuring quality assurance in projects is paramount to achieving successful outcomes and maintaining client satisfaction. This phase of project management involves the systematic review of processes and deliverables to identify and rectify any deficiencies or deviations from established standards. Quality assurance encompasses a proactive approach, where every stage of the project is meticulously monitored for adherence to predefined benchmarks. A comprehensive quality assurance plan should be established at the outset of the project, outlining the criteria for quality measurement, the responsibilities of team members, and the methods for identifying and addressing non-conformances. This anticipatory approach not only minimizes rework and delays but also instills confidence in stakeholders about the project's reliability and effectiveness.

Effective quality assurance requires clear communication channels among team members and stakeholders, enabling the timely resolution of issues and alignment with expectations. Metrics for evaluating quality need to be defined objectively, incorporating both quantitative and qualitative parameters. Additionally, regular audits and reviews should be conducted to ensure that the project is on track and meeting the specified quality standards. Leveraging technological advancements, such as automated testing and monitoring tools, can streamline the quality assurance process and provide real-time insights into potential areas of concern.

Continuous improvement within the project team ensures that lessons learned from previous projects are integrated into the quality assurance practices, preventing recurrent errors and promoting innovation. Emphasizing the importance of quality assurance not only reinforces the commitment to delivering high-quality results but also fosters a reputation for reliability and excellence, setting the stage for long-term success and repeat business. By prioritizing quality throughout the project lifecycle, organizations can demonstrate their dedication to exceeding customer expectations and driving sustainable growth. Ultimately, integrating robust quality assurance practices into project management is essential for mitigating risks, enhancing operational efficiency, and achieving superior project outcomes.

Communication Strategies in Projects

Effective communication lies at the heart of successful project management. It is the cornerstone that ensures all project stakeholders are aligned, informed, and engaged throughout the project lifecycle. The dynamics of a project team hinge on open and clear communication channels, which facilitate the exchange of ideas, feedback, and critical information. In this section, we will look into the essential communication strategies that can elevate project performance and drive success.

One key aspect of communication in projects is establishing a robust communication plan early in the project initiation phase. This plan outlines the methods, frequency, and protocols for communication among team members, stakeholders, and external parties. By defining the communication channels and expectations upfront, project managers can mitigate misunderstandings and ensure that everyone stays on the same page. Furthermore, the plan should account for various communication preferences and needs of different stakeholders, considering factors such as cultural diversity and remote work setups.

Effective project communication involves active listening and fostering an environment where team members feel heard and valued. This not only promotes trust and collaboration but also encourages innovative problem-solving and idea generation. Project leaders should advocate for transparent and open dialogue, where concerns and challenges can be addressed constructively, promoting a culture of continuous improvement and learning within the project team.

Another critical consideration in communication strategies is the use of technology to streamline and enhance project communication. Adopting collaborative tools, project management software, and virtual communication platforms can facilitate real-time information sharing, task tracking, and document management. Leveraging such technologies can also bridge geographical gaps and enable seamless communication among distributed or remote teams, thereby improving overall project efficiency and reducing the likelihood of miscommunication.

Project managers should prioritize regular status updates and progress reports to keep stakeholders informed about project milestones, deliverables, and potential risks.

Transparency in reporting fosters accountability and instills confidence in the project's trajectory. To further optimize communication, utilizing visual aids such as charts, graphs, and dashboards can convey complex data and project insights in a visually accessible manner, ensuring that stakeholders grasp the essential information effectively and make informed decisions.

Effective communication strategies are integral to project success, facilitating alignment, engagement, and transparency among all involved parties. By prioritizing open channels of communication, leveraging technology, and nurturing a culture of active listening, project managers can drive smoother execution, mitigate risks, and uphold stakeholder satisfaction.

Technology in Project Management

In the rapidly evolving landscape of project management, technology has emerged as a game-changer, revolutionizing the way projects are initiated, executed, and monitored. The integration of innovative technological tools and platforms has significantly enhanced the efficiency, transparency, and collaboration within project teams. By leveraging technology, project managers can streamline processes, optimize resource allocation, and mitigate potential risks. One of the primary advantages of integrating technology into project management is the ability to centralize project information and documentation, providing real-time accessibility to all stakeholders. Through cloud-based project management systems, teams can seamlessly collaborate, share updates, and access critical project data from anywhere in the world. Furthermore, the utilization of project management software and tools facilitates the automation of repetitive tasks, enabling team members to focus on more strategic and value-driven activities.

The implementation of advanced analytics and reporting features empowers project managers to make data-driven decisions, identify trends, and anticipate potential bottlenecks. These insights not only enhance project performance but also enable proactive risk management and issue resolution. The adoption of communication and collaboration tools such as video conferencing, instant messaging, and virtual workspaces promotes seamless interaction among dispersed project teams, bringing a cohesive and connected work environment. The integration of technology also plays a pivotal role in enhancing stakeholder engagement and satisfaction by providing transparent and real-time project progress updates. From agile project management methodologies to virtual reality simulations for complex project planning, the opportunities for leveraging technology in project management are extensive and diverse. Embracing these technological advancements empowers project managers to drive innovation, optimize decision-making, and achieve greater project success. As the digital landscape continues to evolve, staying abreast of emerging technologies and their application in project management is essential for maintaining a competitive edge and delivering exceptional results.

Closing Projects Successfully

The successful closure of a project is critical to ensure that the intended objectives have been met and deliverables have been achieved. This phase encompasses various activities that need to be carefully orchestrated to bring the project to a conclusion with maximum effectiveness.

One vital aspect of closing a project is the formal acceptance of deliverables by the client or stakeholders. This involves a comprehensive review of all project outcomes, ensuring that they align with the initial project scope and requirements. It may also involve obtaining formal sign-off on the completion of the project's deliverables.

Final documentation and reporting play a significant role in the project closure process. This includes creating a comprehensive project closure report, which outlines the overall performance, achievements, challenges faced, lessons learned, and recommendations for future projects. This report serves as a valuable knowledge base for organizational learning and continuous improvement.

It is essential to conduct a thorough evaluation of the project against its original goals and success criteria. This assessment helps in identifying areas of accomplishment, as well as any deviations or shortcomings, enabling the team to reflect on their performance and make necessary adjustments for future endeavors.

Engaging in a structured handover process is crucial to ensure a smooth transition of project deliverables, responsibilities, and knowledge to the relevant stakeholders and operational teams. This transfer of ownership should be meticulously planned to mitigate any disruptions once the project is formally closed.

Equally important is the recognition and celebration of the efforts put forth by the project team throughout the entire project lifecycle. Acknowledging the hard work and dedication of team members fosters a positive work culture and motivates individuals to strive for excellence in future projects.

Simultaneously, an effective project closure also involves tying up any loose ends, including financial matters, contracts, and supplier relationships, to achieve a seamless and satisfactory conclusion to the project's lifecycle.

The ability to close a project successfully not only reflects the project management team's capability but also contributes to the organization's reputation and future prospects. It signifies professionalism, attention to detail, and commitment to delivering quality outcomes.

Strategies for Self-Improvement

Project management is a critical skill for leaders, involving the ability to plan, execute, and close projects effectively. Below are the top five project management challenges and strategies for becoming a problem solver:

1. Scope Creep

Challenge: Managing project scope and preventing uncontrolled changes that can derail the project.

Self-Development Strategies:

Scope Definition:

- *Clear Objectives*: Learn to set clear project objectives and deliverables. Study project scope management techniques and frameworks.
- *Requirements Gathering*: Enhance your skills in gathering and documenting detailed requirements from stakeholders.

Change Control:

- *Change Management*: Take courses on change management and learn how to implement a robust change control process.
- *Stakeholder Communication*: Develop effective communication strategies to

keep stakeholders informed about scope changes and their impact.

Project Charter:

- *Comprehensive Documentation*: Create comprehensive project charters that clearly define scope, objectives, and boundaries.

- *Sign-off Procedures*: Establish sign-off procedures for scope changes to ensure stakeholder agreement and control.

2. Time Management and Deadlines

Challenge: Meeting project deadlines and managing time effectively to keep the project on track.

Self-Development Strategies:

Scheduling Techniques:

- *Gantt Charts and Critical Path:* Learn to use Gantt charts, Critical Path Method (CPM), and other scheduling tools to plan and track project timelines.

- *Time Estimation:* Improve your time estimation skills through practice and by studying estimation techniques such as PERT (Program Evaluation and Review Technique).

Task Prioritization:

- *Prioritization Frameworks:* Use prioritization frameworks like the MoSCoW method (Must have, Should have, Could have, Won't have) to prioritize tasks.

- *Agile Methodologies:* Study agile project management methodologies that focus on iterative progress and time-boxed sprints.

Productivity Tools:

- *Project Management Software*: Get proficient in project management software like Microsoft Project, Asana, Trello, or Jira to manage tasks and timelines effectively.

- *Time Blocking:* Implement time blocking techniques to allocate specific periods for focused work on high-priority tasks.

3. Resource Allocation

Challenge: Efficiently allocating and managing resources (people, budget, equipment) to ensure project success.

Self-Development Strategies:

Resource Planning:

- *Resource Management Courses*: Take courses on resource planning and management to learn how to allocate resources effectively.

- *Resource Allocation Tools*: Use resource allocation tools and techniques, such as RACI charts (Responsible, Accountable, Consulted, Informed) and resource leveling.

Budget Management:

- *Budgeting Skills*: Enhance your budgeting skills by studying financial management and cost control techniques.

- *Contingency Planning:* Develop contingency plans to manage unexpected changes in resource availability or costs.

Team Management:

- *Skill Development*: Invest in developing your team's skills to ensure they are well-equipped to handle project tasks.

- *Delegation:* Practice effective delegation to ensure tasks are assigned to the right people with the right skills.

4. Risk Management

Challenge: Identifying, assessing, and mitigating risks to prevent project failure.

Self-Development Strategies:

Risk Assessment:

- *Risk Management Training*: Take courses on risk management frameworks and techniques, such as SWOT analysis and Risk Breakdown Structure (RBS).

- *Quantitative and Qualitative Analysis*: Learn both quantitative and qualitative risk analysis methods to assess potential project risks.

Risk Mitigation:

- *Mitigation Strategies*: Develop strategies for mitigating identified risks, including contingency planning and preventive measures.

- *Scenario Planning:* Practice scenario planning to anticipate and prepare for potential risks and their impacts on the project.

Monitoring and Control:

- *Risk Registers:* Maintain a risk register to track identified risks, their status, and mitigation actions.
- *Regular Reviews:* Conduct regular risk review meetings with your team to assess new risks and update mitigation plans.

5. Stakeholder Management

Challenge: Engaging and managing stakeholders effectively to ensure their needs and expectations are met.

Self-Development Strategies:

Stakeholder Analysis:

- *Identification and Analysis*: Learn techniques for identifying stakeholders and analyzing their interests, influence, and impact on the project.
- *Engagement Strategies:* Develop strategies for engaging stakeholders based on their level of interest and influence.

Communication Skills:

- *Effective Communication:* Improve your communication skills through training and practice. Focus on clarity, active listening, and tailored messaging.

- *Regular Updates:* Establish regular communication channels, such as status reports and meetings, to keep stakeholders informed and engaged.

Conflict Resolution:

- *Conflict Management Training:* Take courses on conflict management and negotiation to handle stakeholder disagreements and conflicts effectively.

- *Mediation Skills*: Develop mediation skills to facilitate discussions and find mutually acceptable solutions to stakeholder issues.

7

SALES AND MARKETING

Sales and marketing are the art and science of creating value and building connections. By understanding the needs of your audience and crafting compelling narratives, you not only drive growth but also forge lasting relationships that are the heart of any successful enterprise."

Understanding the Sales Funnel

The sales funnel is a foundational concept in marketing and sales that *represents the journey a potential customer takes from being aware of a product or service to making a purchase.* It consists of several stages, starting with the widest part of the funnel where the customers first become aware of the product or service. This initial stage is known as the *'awareness'* stage. The next stage is *'interest,'* where potential customers show interest in the offering and seek more information. Subsequently, they move to the *'decision'* stage, where they evaluate different options before making a purchasing decision. Finally, the *'action'* stage is where the actual purchase takes place.

Awareness ▶ Interest ▶ Decision ▶ Action

Understanding this process is crucial for businesses as it helps them tailor their marketing and sales strategies to address the needs and concerns of potential customers at each stage of the funnel. By developing targeted content and messaging, businesses can effectively guide customers through the sales funnel, ultimately leading to a higher conversion rate and increased sales.

The sales funnel provides valuable insights into customer behavior and preferences, enabling businesses to refine their marketing and sales efforts. With a clear understanding of the sales funnel, businesses can optimize their resources and focus on activities that yield the highest return on investment. In today's competitive market, mastering the art of guiding customers through the sales funnel is essential for sustained growth and profitability.

Effective Sales Techniques

Sales are the lifeblood of any business, and mastering effective sales techniques is crucial for driving revenue and growth. The essential strategies and practices can help you excel in sales, build strong customer relationships, and achieve your sales targets.

1. Building Rapport:

Personal Connection: Establish a personal connection with potential clients. Show genuine interest in their needs and challenges to build trust and rapport.

Active Listening: Practice active listening by fully focusing on the client's words, asking clarifying questions, and showing empathy. Understanding their needs helps tailor your pitch effectively.

2. Understanding Customer Needs:

Needs Assessment: Conduct thorough needs assessments to identify the specific pain points and requirements of your clients. Use open-ended questions to gather detailed information.

Value Proposition: Clearly articulate your product or service's value proposition, highlighting how it addresses the client's needs and provides solutions to their problems.

3. Effective Communication:

Clear and Concise Messaging: Communicate your value proposition clearly and concisely. Avoid jargon and ensure that your message is easily understood.

Storytelling: Use storytelling to make your pitch more engaging and relatable. Share success stories and case studies that demonstrate the effectiveness of your solution.

4. Handling Objections:

Anticipate Objections: Prepare for common objections in advance and develop responses that address them effectively. Understanding common concerns can help you build stronger arguments.

Empathy and Understanding: Address objections with empathy and understanding. Acknowledge the client's concerns and provide clear, fact-based responses to alleviate their doubts.

5. Closing Techniques:

Assumptive Close: Act as if the client has already decided to buy. Use phrases like "When we start..." to create a sense of inevitability.

Urgency and Scarcity: Create a sense of urgency by highlighting limited availability or time-sensitive offers. This can encourage clients to make a decision promptly.

Trial Close: Use trial closes to gauge the client's readiness to buy. Questions like "How does this solution fit with your current needs?" can help you understand their mindset.

6. Follow-Up and Relationship Building:

Consistent Follow-Up: Follow up consistently with potential clients. Regular communication shows your commitment and keeps your solution top of mind.

Long-Term Relationships: Focus on building long-term relationships rather than just closing a single sale. Provide ongoing value and support to foster loyalty and repeat business.

7. Leveraging Technology:

CRM Systems: Utilize Customer Relationship Management (CRM) systems to track interactions, manage leads, and analyze sales data. CRM tools help streamline the sales process and improve efficiency.

Sales Analytics: Use sales analytics to identify trends, measure performance, and optimize your sales strategies. Data-driven insights can guide decision-making and improve outcomes.

8. Continuous Improvement:

Sales Training: Invest in regular sales training and professional development. Stay updated on the latest sales techniques, tools, and industry trends.

Performance Review: Regularly review your sales performance and seek feedback from clients and colleagues. Identify areas for improvement and implement changes to enhance your effectiveness.

The Art of Persuasion in Sales

In the realm of sales, the art of persuasion is an indispensable skill that separates the average salesperson from the truly exceptional ones. *It involves mastering the ability to influence and convince potential customers to make a purchase by effectively addressing their needs and concerns.* The art of persuasion encompasses various psychological and communicative techniques that can be employed throughout the sales process. *One fundamental aspect of persuasion is the ability to actively listen to the customer, understand their pain points, and tailor the presentation of products or services to meet their specific requirements. Storytelling* can be a powerful tool, as it allows salespeople to connect with prospects on an emotional level, making the benefits of the offering more tangible and relatable. *Understanding the principles of behavioral psychology, such as social proof and reciprocity, further enhances the persuasive capabilities of sales professionals.*

Building rapport and establishing trust are crucial components of persuasion, as customers are more likely to buy from someone they trust and feel a connection with. Utilizing nonverbal cues, mirroring body language, and employing persuasive language patterns all contribute to creating a positive and influential interaction. The use of compelling evidence, testimonials, and case studies can strengthen the persuasiveness of sales pitches, providing tangible proofs of the value and effectiveness of the offering.

Successful persuasion also involves handling objections with finesse, transforming them into opportunities to further demonstrate the product's or service's benefits. However, ethical considerations must always underpin the art of persuasion in sales, ensuring that the process remains honest, transparent, and ultimately beneficial for the customer. By mastering the art of persuasion, sales professionals can forge lasting connections, build a loyal customer base, and achieve remarkable success in driving sales and revenue.

Creating Compelling Marketing Campaigns

Regardless of the industry or market, compelling marketing campaigns play a pivotal role in establishing a brand's position and driving consumer engagement. *A successful campaign captures the audience's attention, generates interest, and ultimately leads to desired actions, such as product purchases or brand advocacy.* To create truly compelling marketing campaigns, it is essential to understand the target audience, identify their needs and preferences, and craft messages that resonate with them on an emotional level.

A deep comprehension of market trends, competitive landscape, and marketing channels is crucial for delivering effective campaigns. When developing a campaign, it's vital to integrate a creative concept that aligns with the brand's identity, values, and strategic objectives. This concept serves as the foundation for all marketing materials and communications, ensuring consistency and coherence across various touchpoints. Whether it's through captivating visuals, impactful storytelling, or innovative strategies, a compelling marketing campaign has the power to drive brand awareness, influence purchasing behavior, and foster lasting connections with consumers.

Leveraging cutting-edge technologies and digital platforms, marketers can deploy personalized, targeted campaigns that resonate with specific segments of their audience, maximizing impact and return on investment. However, regardless of the tools and mediums used, the authenticity and relevance of the campaign message are paramount. Engaging content that offers value, solves problems, or entertains the audience forms the cornerstone of compelling marketing campaigns. Furthermore, the evaluation and measurement of campaign performance are integral in refining future efforts. By analyzing key performance indicators, gathering consumer feedback, and adapting strategies based on insights, marketers can continuously improve the effectiveness of their campaigns, ensuring relevance and resonance in an ever-evolving marketplace.

Creating compelling marketing campaigns requires a harmonious blend of art and science, leveraging creativity and innovation while staying grounded in data-driven strategies and consumer insights. With a thorough understanding of the target audience, a clear brand voice, and an agile approach to adaptation, marketers can craft compelling campaigns that leave a lasting impression and drive meaningful business outcomes.

Digital Marketing Trends

Digital marketing continues to evolve at a rapid pace, ushering in new trends that redefine how brands engage with their target audiences. One of the most transformative trends in digital marketing is the rise of personalized and targeted advertising. With the help of advanced data analytics and machine learning algorithms, marketers can now tailor their content and advertisements to individual consumers based on their behaviors, preferences, and past interactions. This level of personalization not only enhances the customer experience but also drives higher conversion rates and return on investment.

Another pivotal trend is the increasing emphasis on video content. With the ever-growing popularity of platforms like YouTube, TikTok, and Instagram, video has become a dominant form of communication for brands, offering a more immersive and engaging way to connect with consumers. As attention spans shorten, marketers are leveraging short-form videos, live streams, and interactive content to capture and retain audience interest. Furthermore, the impact of influencer marketing cannot be overstated. Collaborating with social media influencers who have a loyal following allows brands to tap into established communities and leverage authentic endorsements, thereby amplifying their reach and credibility. The advent of *artificial intelligence (AI) and chatbots* has revolutionized customer engagement. AI-powered chatbots enable real-time, personalized interactions with customers, providing instant support and recommendations while gathering valuable customer data. Beyond that, the evolution of *augmented reality (AR) and virtual reality (VR)* technologies presents exciting opportunities for immersive brand experiences and product demonstrations. These emerging technologies can transport consumers into captivating virtual environments, enabling them to interact with products in entirely new ways.

Sustainability and corporate social responsibility are emerging as influential factors in digital marketing. Consumers are increasingly drawn to brands that demonstrate environmental stewardship and ethical business practices, prompting marketers to integrate sustainability narratives into their digital campaigns. By aligning with eco-friendly initiatives and social causes, brands can forge deeper emotional connections with socially conscious consumers. As digital marketing continues to evolve, staying abreast of these trends is crucial for marketers seeking to remain competitive and relevant in an ever-changing landscape.

Customer Relationship Management

Customer relationship management (CRM) strategies encompass a multifaceted approach to understanding and addressing the needs of your customer base. At the core of effective CRM lies the ability to listen to customers, anticipate their requirements, and provide personalized solutions that resonate with their unique preferences and expectations.

CRM extends beyond a mere transactional relationship; it is about building long-term engagement and loyalty. By leveraging data analytics and customer feedback, businesses can gain valuable insights into customer behavior, enabling them to tailor their product offerings and communication strategies effectively. This personalized approach not only enhances customer satisfaction but also drives repeat purchases and referrals, contributing significantly to the bottom line.

Implementing robust CRM systems empowers organizations to streamline their processes, optimize resource allocation, and identify opportunities for cross-selling and upselling. By centralizing customer data and interactions, businesses can deliver targeted marketing campaigns, offer personalized promotions, and proactively address any issues or concerns raised by customers.

In an era where word-of-mouth and online reviews carry substantial weight, nurturing positive customer relationships can be a powerful differentiator. Engaging with customers on various touchpoints, whether through social media, email, or support channels, allows businesses to demonstrate their commitment to customer satisfaction and build trust. Satisfied customers are more likely to become brand advocates, actively promoting the company's products and services within their own networks.

Good customer relationship management transcends mere transactional exchanges to cultivate meaningful connections and drive sustainable business growth. By prioritizing customer-centric approaches, businesses can position themselves as trusted partners, secure customer loyalty, and gain a competitive edge in the market.

Creating Effective Marketing Strategy

A well-crafted marketing strategy is essential for attracting and retaining customers, building brand awareness, and driving business growth. Below is an outline of the key components of an effective marketing strategy and provides practical steps to develop and implement it successfully.

1. Market Research:

Understanding Your Market: Conduct thorough market research to understand your target audience, industry trends, and competitive landscape. Use surveys, focus groups, and data analysis to gather insights.

Customer Personas: Develop detailed customer personas that represent your ideal customers. Understand their demographics, preferences, behaviors, and pain points.

2. Defining Your Unique Selling Proposition (USP):

Differentiation: Identify what sets your product or service apart from competitors. Clearly articulate your Unique Selling Proposition (USP) to highlight your competitive advantages.

Value Proposition: Communicate the unique value your product or service provides. Focus on the benefits and outcomes that matter most to your target audience.

3. Setting Clear Objectives:

SMART Goals: Establish Specific, Measurable, Achievable, Relevant, and Time-bound (SMART) marketing goals. Clear objectives provide direction and enable you to measure success.

Key Performance Indicators (KPIs): Define KPIs to track the effectiveness of your marketing efforts. Common KPIs include lead generation, conversion rates, customer acquisition cost, and return on investment (ROI).

4. Crafting Your Marketing Message:

Consistent Messaging: Develop a consistent marketing message that resonates with your target audience. Ensure that all marketing materials align with your brand voice and values.

Emotional Appeal: Create marketing messages that evoke emotions and connect with your audience on a personal level. Emotional appeal can enhance brand loyalty and engagement.

5. Choosing the Right Marketing Channels:

Digital Marketing: Leverage digital marketing channels such as social media, email marketing, content marketing, and search engine optimization (SEO). Each channel has unique advantages and can reach different segments of your audience.

Traditional Marketing: Consider traditional marketing methods like print advertising, direct mail, and events. Depending on your audience, traditional channels may still be highly effective.

6. Content Marketing:

Creating Valuable Content: Produce high-quality, valuable content that addresses your audience's needs and interests. Blog posts, videos, infographics, and whitepapers can educate, inform, and engage your audience.

Content Distribution: Distribute your content through various channels to maximize reach. Share content on social media, through email newsletters, and on your website.

7. Social Media Marketing:

Platform Selection: Choose the right social media platforms based on where your target audience spends their time. Focus your efforts on the platforms that offer the best engagement opportunities.

Engagement Strategies: Develop strategies to engage your audience through social media. Use a mix of organic posts, paid advertising, and interactive content to build relationships and drive traffic.

8. Measuring and Analyzing Results:

Analytics Tools: Use analytics tools to track the performance of your marketing campaigns. Google Analytics, social media analytics, and email marketing platforms provide valuable data.

Adjusting Strategies: Analyze the results of your marketing efforts and make data-driven adjustments. Continuously optimize your strategies based on what works best.

9. Budgeting and Resource Allocation:

Marketing Budget: Develop a marketing budget that aligns with your overall business goals. Allocate resources to the most effective channels and tactics.

Resource Management: Ensure that you have the necessary resources, including personnel and technology, to execute your marketing strategy effectively.

10. Continuous Improvement:

Feedback and Adaptation: Gather feedback from customers, analyze market trends, and stay updated on industry developments. Continuously adapt your marketing strategy to stay relevant and effective.

Learning and Development: Invest in ongoing learning and professional development for your marketing team. Staying current with the latest marketing techniques and tools ensures continued success.

Pricing Strategies for Maximum Profit

Setting the right price for a product or service is a critical decision that significantly impacts the success of any business. Pricing strategies play a vital role in achieving maximum profit and establishing a competitive edge in the market. To determine the most effective pricing strategy, businesses must consider various factors such as production costs, customer demand, competitor pricing, and perceived value. When developing a pricing strategy, it's essential to strike a balance between generating revenue and maintaining a loyal customer base.

One approach to pricing is *cost-plus pricing*, which involves calculating the total production cost of an item and adding a markup to set the selling price. While cost-plus pricing provides a straightforward method for determining prices, it may not necessarily reflect the actual value perceived by customers. In contrast, *value-based pricing* focuses on aligning the price with the perceived value of the product or service in the eyes of the customer. This approach requires a deep understanding of customer preferences, market dynamics, and the unique selling proposition of the product.

Dynamic pricing is another innovative strategy that leverages real-time data and market conditions to adjust prices for optimal profitability. By employing dynamic pricing algorithms, businesses can optimize prices based on factors such as demand fluctuations, competitor pricing, and customer behavior. However, implementing dynamic pricing requires careful consideration of ethical implications and customer perception to avoid backlash.

Bundle pricing and psychological pricing tactics can influence customer buying behavior and enhance sales performance. Bundling complementary products together at a discounted price can create perceived value and encourage customers to make larger purchases. Similarly, utilizing psychological pricing techniques, such as *charm pricing (setting prices just below a round number) or prestige pricing (positioning products as luxury items)*, can impact consumer perception and willingness to pay.

The key to successful pricing strategies lies in continuous monitoring, analysis, and adaptation. Businesses need to stay attuned to market trends, gather customer feedback, and be willing to adjust their pricing approaches to remain competitive and maximize profitability. Transparency and honesty in pricing create trust and strengthens the relationship between businesses and their customer base. By meticulously evaluating and implementing pricing strategies, businesses can effectively drive revenue, sustain growth, and achieve long-term success.

Sales Metrics and KPIs

In sales and marketing, understanding and effectively utilizing **sales metrics** and **key performance indicators (KPIs)** is crucial for success. Sales metrics are quantifiable measures that assess a company's sales performance and help to evaluate the effectiveness of sales strategies. Meanwhile, KPIs are specific, measurable values used to track progress towards business goals. By focusing on these metrics and KPIs, businesses can gain valuable insights into their sales processes, identify areas for improvement, and make data-driven decisions.

One essential sales metric is *revenue,* which indicates the total income generated from sales activities. Monitoring revenue trends over time can reveal the impact of pricing strategies, market demand, and customer preferences. Another vital metric is the *sales growth rate,* which measures the percentage increase in sales over a specified period. Understanding sales growth helps businesses gauge their market expansion and identify opportunities for further development. Keeping a close eye on the *customer acquisition cost (CAC)* is critical for assessing the efficiency of sales and marketing efforts. CAC calculates the expenses incurred to acquire a new customer and provides valuable insights into the return on investment. Tracking the *conversion rate* allows businesses to measure the percentage of prospects that become paying customers. Understanding the factors influencing conversion rates can lead to targeted improvements in sales strategies and customer interactions.

In conjunction with sales metrics, identifying and *utilizing effective KPIs* is vital for aligning sales and marketing activities with broader business objectives. *Examples of sales KPIs include monthly sales growth, customer lifetime value, sales qualified leads, and win rate.* These KPIs provide actionable insights into the effectiveness of sales initiatives, customer loyalty, and the overall health of the sales pipeline. By leveraging robust sales metrics and KPIs, businesses can optimize their sales and marketing strategies, enhance decision-making, and drive sustainable growth. Furthermore, implementing a comprehensive performance management system that includes regular monitoring and analysis of these metrics and KPIs is essential for fostering a culture of continuous improvement and accountability within the sales team. By empowering sales professionals with the right tools and insights, companies can maximize their sales potential, achieve sustainable revenue growth, and maintain a competitive edge in the market.

Leveraging Social-Media

Social media has evolved into one of the most powerful marketing tools in today's digital age. *Leveraging social media effectively can significantly enhance a company's reach and engagement with its target audience.* Platforms like Facebook, Instagram, X, LinkedIn, and TikTok offer unique opportunities for businesses to connect with potential customers and build brand awareness. One of the key advantages of using social media for marketing is its cost-effectiveness. Compared to traditional advertising channels, social media platforms typically offer lower costs and higher levels of targeting, allowing businesses of all sizes to compete on a level playing field.

The real-time nature of social media allows companies to engage in immediate interactions with their audience, providing a valuable means of gathering feedback and addressing customer concerns. Successful social media marketing strategies often involve creating compelling visual content, such as videos and infographics, to capture the attention of users scrolling through their feeds. Furthermore, the use of hashtags and trending topics can help boost visibility and attract a larger audience. It's essential for businesses to maintain an active presence on social media by consistently posting engaging content and participating in relevant conversations within their industry.

Another aspect of leveraging social media involves understanding the analytics and insights provided by these platforms. By analyzing metrics such as reach, engagement, and conversion rates, companies can refine their marketing strategies and make data-driven decisions to optimize their social media performance. Social media advertising offers highly targeted options to reach specific demographics, thereby maximizing the impact of promotional campaigns. It's crucial for businesses to stay updated on the latest trends and features across various social media platforms in order to adapt and capitalize on new opportunities. By effectively leveraging social media, businesses can cultivate a loyal online community, drive traffic to their websites, and ultimately increase sales and revenue.

Negotiation Techniques

Negotiation is a crucial skill in the world of sales and marketing. It requires a delicate balance of assertiveness, empathy, and strategic thinking. *Effective negotiation techniques can make the difference between a successful deal and a lost opportunity.* In the realm of sales and marketing, negotiations often occur with clients, partners, vendors, and even within the internal team. To excel in negotiations, one must grasp the art of active listening. Understanding the needs, motivations, and pain points of the other party is essential for aligning proposals and finding mutually beneficial solutions. It's also important to establish clear objectives and boundaries before entering negotiations.

Successful negotiators are adept at creating *win-win outcomes*. This involves finding opportunities where both parties can achieve their goals without feeling compromised. The ability to think creatively and explore alternative solutions is key in reaching such agreements. Being able to remain calm and composed under pressure, especially in high-stakes negotiations, can greatly influence the outcome. Confidence and poise convey a sense of reliability and trustworthiness, which can positively impact the negotiation process.

Understanding various negotiation styles is indispensable in mastering this skill. Whether it's competitive, collaborative, compromising, accommodating, or avoiding, knowing when and how to employ each style is crucial. Flexibility in adapting to different negotiation scenarios is imperative for achieving favorable results. In addition to styles, knowing the cultural nuances and communication norms of the parties involved can significantly affect the negotiation dynamics.

Lastly, preparation plays a pivotal role in successful negotiations. Thoroughly researching the other party, understanding market trends, and anticipating potential objections can provide a competitive advantage. Building rapport, demonstrating credibility, and showcasing value propositions are all vital aspects of effective negotiation. Honing these negotiation skills will not only lead to better deals but also foster stronger and more enduring business relationships.

Ethical Sales Practices

In the world of sales, ethical practices are essential for building long-term relationships and maintaining credibility. Ethical sales practices revolve around transparency, honesty, and integrity in all client interactions. This encompasses representing products or services accurately and truthfully, avoiding deceptive sales tactics, and respecting customer privacy and confidentiality.

Ethical sales professionals prioritize understanding the customer's needs and providing valuable solutions that align with those needs. They refrain from pressuring clients into making purchases they do not need or cannot afford, striving instead to foster trust and demonstrate genuine care for the customer's best interests. By prioritizing ethics in sales, professionals not only build stronger rapport with clients, but also contribute to the establishment of a positive brand image for their organization.

Ethical sales practices extend to pricing strategies. Sales professionals aim to offer fair and competitive prices without engaging in price gouging or exploitative tactics. They are transparent about costs and ensure that customers fully comprehend the value they are receiving for their investment. Additionally, ethical sales involve clear communication regarding refund policies, warranties, and any associated terms and conditions, ensuring that customers are well-informed and feel secure in their purchasing decisions.

When it comes to ethical sales practices, data privacy and security are paramount considerations. Sales professionals must handle customer data responsibly, ensuring compliance with data protection regulations and safeguarding sensitive information from unauthorized access. This entails obtaining explicit consent for data usage, securing digital platforms, and implementing robust cybersecurity measures to protect customer information.

Ethical sales practices encompass accountability and professionalism. Sales professionals take responsibility for their actions, promptly addressing any errors, concerns, or dissatisfaction on the part of the customer. By upholding high standards of professionalism and accountability, sales professionals reinforce trust and credibility, setting a benchmark for ethical conduct within the industry.

Ethical sales practices are not only morally imperative but also beneficial for sustainable business growth. When organizations prioritize ethicality in their sales approach, they cultivate enduring relationships with customers and establish a reputation for integrity and reliability. Such practices lay the foundation for long-term success by fostering loyalty, driving positive word-of-mouth referrals, and differentiating the organization from competitors.

Strategies for Self-Improvement

Sales and marketing are critical functions in any business, and leaders in these areas often face a range of challenges. Here are the sales and marketing challenges and strategies for overcoming them:

1. Understanding Customer Needs

Challenge: Identifying and understanding the evolving needs and preferences of customers.

Self-Development Strategies:

Customer Research:

- *Market Research Training*: Take courses on market research methods to learn how to gather and analyze customer data effectively.

- *Customer Surveys and Interviews*: Practice designing and conducting customer surveys and interviews to gain direct insights into customer needs.

Data Analysis Skills:

- *Analytics Tools*: Learn to use data analytics tools like Google Analytics, CRM software, and BI platforms to track customer behavior and preferences.

- *Segmentation*: Study customer segmentation techniques to categorize customers based on various criteria and tailor marketing strategies accordingly.

Empathy and Listening:

- *Active Listening*: Develop active listening skills to better understand customer feedback and concerns.

- *Customer Journey Mapping*: Learn to create customer journey maps to visualize and improve the customer experience.

2. Generating Leads and Converting Them into Sales

Challenge: Effectively generating leads and converting them into paying customers.

Self-Development Strategies:

Lead Generation Techniques:

- *Inbound Marketing*: Study inbound marketing strategies, including content marketing, SEO, and social media marketing, to attract and engage potential customers.

- *Outbound Marketing*: Learn about outbound marketing techniques such as email marketing, cold calling, and direct mail.

Sales Skills:

- *Sales Training*: Attend sales training programs to improve your selling techniques, from prospecting to closing deals.
- *Negotiation Skills*: Enhance your negotiation skills through practice and training to close deals more effectively.

Sales Funnel Management:

- *Funnel Optimization*: Learn to optimize the sales funnel by analyzing each stage and identifying areas for improvement.
- *CRM Systems*: Get proficient in using CRM systems to track leads, manage customer relationships, and streamline sales processes.

3. Differentiating from Competitors

Challenge: Standing out in a crowded market and differentiating your products or services from competitors.

Self-Development Strategies:

Competitive Analysis:

- *SWOT Analysis*: Conduct SWOT analyses (Strengths, Weaknesses, Opportunities, Threats) to understand your competitive position.

- *Benchmarking:* Study competitors' strategies and performance to identify opportunities for differentiation.

Unique Value Proposition:

- *Value Proposition Design*: Learn to develop a strong value proposition that clearly communicates the unique benefits of your products or services.
- *Brand Positioning*: Study brand positioning techniques to effectively position your brand in the market.

Innovation and Creativity:

- *Creative Thinking*: Engage in creative thinking exercises and brainstorming sessions to generate innovative ideas.
- *Product Development*: Stay informed about the latest trends and technologies in your industry to innovate and improve your offerings.

4. Adapting to Digital Transformation

Challenge: Keeping up with digital transformation and leveraging new technologies in sales and marketing.

Self-Development Strategies:

Digital Marketing Skills:

- *Online Courses*: Take online courses in digital marketing, including social media marketing, email marketing, and content marketing.

- *Certifications:* Pursue certifications like Google Ads, Google Analytics, or HubSpot's Inbound Marketing Certification.

Technology Proficiency:

- *Marketing Automation*: Learn to use marketing automation tools to streamline campaigns and improve efficiency.

- *Analytics and AI*: Study the application of analytics and artificial intelligence in sales and marketing to enhance decision-making and personalization.

Continuous Learning:

- *Webinars and Workshops*: Regularly attend webinars and workshops on digital marketing trends and technologies.

- *Industry Publications:* Stay updated with industry publications, blogs, and podcasts that cover digital transformation topics.

5. Building and Maintaining Customer Relationships

Challenge: Building strong, lasting relationships with customers and maintaining high levels of customer satisfaction and loyalty.

Self-Development Strategies:

Customer Relationship Management:

- *CRM Training*: Get trained in using CRM systems to manage customer interactions and data effectively.

- *Personalization:* Learn techniques for personalizing customer interactions to enhance engagement and loyalty.

Customer Service Skills:

- *Customer Service Training*: Attend customer service training to improve your ability to handle customer inquiries, complaints, and feedback.

- *Empathy and Communication*: Develop strong empathy and communication skills to build trust and rapport with customers.

Loyalty Programs:

- *Design and Implementation*: Study how to design and implement effective customer loyalty programs that reward repeat business.

- *Customer Feedback*: Implement regular feedback mechanisms to gather insights on customer satisfaction and areas for improvement.

8

ADAPTABILITY & RESILIENCE

"Adaptability and resilience are the twin pillars of enduring success. Embrace change with flexibility and face adversity with strength, for it is through these qualities that we not only survive but thrive in an ever-evolving world."

Understanding Adaptability

As businesses navigate through a rapidly evolving landscape, it becomes imperative to understand the concept of adaptability and its significance in maintaining relevance and competitiveness. We will discuss the key forces and trends that shape today's business environment, necessitating a paradigm shift towards flexibility and agility. The seismic shifts in technology, consumer behavior, and global economic dynamics underscore the need for organizations to embrace change as a constant. By examining these influential factors, we can grasp the urgency for adaptability and appreciate its role in fostering sustainability and growth.

The Psychology of Resilience

Resilience is all about *mental strength*. Resilience is a fundamental aspect of navigating the challenges and uncertainties present in today's dynamic business landscape. Beyond mere adaptability, *it encompasses the ability to bounce back from setbacks, to endure hardship, and to maintain clarity and focus amid turbulent times*. The psychology of resilience looks into the intricate workings of the human mind and its capacity to overcome adversity. At its core, building mental strength involves understanding the mechanisms that drive resilience and leveraging them to fortify one's psychological resilience. *Psychologists assert that resilience is not an innate trait but rather a skill that can be nurtured and cultivated, akin to a muscle that grows stronger with each challenge faced.* It involves developing a growth mindset, characterized by an unwavering belief in one's ability to learn, grow, and adapt in the face of adversity.

Nurturing emotional intelligence plays a pivotal role in developing resilience. Embracing emotional agility and mindfulness allows individuals to process and manage their emotions effectively, enabling them to respond resiliently to adversity. Building mental strength also hinges on cultivating a sense of purpose and meaning. When individuals align their actions with a strong sense of purpose, they develop a reservoir of strength and determination that propels them forward despite obstacles.

The cultivation of optimism and hope serves as a potent catalyst for resilience. Researchers have found that individuals who maintain a positive outlook and cultivate hopefulness are more adept at navigating challenges and bouncing back from setbacks. The power of social connections cannot be underestimated in the realm of resilience. Building a robust support network and fostering meaningful relationships bolster one's ability to weather storms and emerge stronger. By surrounding oneself with supportive and nurturing individuals, one can draw strength and guidance during tumultuous times. In essence, the psychology of resilience underscores the transformative potential within each individual to build and fortify their mental strength, equipping them with the resilience needed to thrive amidst uncertainty and change.

Adapting to Market Changes with Agility

The ability to adapt to market changes with agility is paramount for staying competitive and relevant. As markets shift and customer preferences change, organizations must be fluid and adept in their responses. This involves closely monitoring industry trends, consumer behavior, and economic fluctuations to proactively identify opportunities and threats. Agile adaptation necessitates a willingness to embrace change and a proactive mindset that thrives on uncertainty. Successful adaptation also demands a deep understanding of the market dynamics, enabling organizations to pivot swiftly while maintaining operational continuity.

Encouraging a culture of innovation and experimentation within the organization encourages adaptive responses to market shifts. Companies that prioritize agility often implement streamlined decision-making processes and promote autonomous decision-making at various levels to facilitate quick adjustments. Embracing technology and digital transformation plays a pivotal role in enhancing organizational agility. Leveraging data analytics, artificial intelligence, and automation empowers businesses to anticipate market changes and respond nimbly. Cross-functional collaboration and open communication channels enable seamless sharing of insights and best practices, fostering an environment conducive to rapid adaptation.

Building strategic partnerships and alliances can provide access to diverse perspectives, resources, and capabilities, augmenting an organization's agility. It's essential to cultivate a dynamic workforce capable of responding to market changes effectively. This includes investing in continuous training and upskilling programs to equip employees with the necessary competencies. *Promoting a mindset that embraces change and sees it as an opportunity for growth is pivotal in ingraining agility into the organizational DNA.* By embracing these principles and practices, organizations can not only weather market changes but also thrive in dynamic environments, positioning themselves as leaders in their respective industries.

Cultivating a Flexible Team Culture

Building a flexible team culture within an organization is paramount to navigating the ever-changing landscape of the business world. A flexible team culture encourages open-mindedness, adaptability, and teamwork, which are essential qualities for thriving in dynamic environments. To cultivate such a culture, leaders must first demonstrate and communicate the value of flexibility to their teams. This can be accomplished by showcasing successful instances where adaptability has resulted in positive outcomes, thereby reinforcing the significance of being responsive to change.

Creating an environment that embraces diverse perspectives and encourages new ideas can lay the groundwork for fostering flexibility within the team. By incorporating different viewpoints and approaches, teams can better adapt to shifting circumstances, ultimately leading to more innovative and effective solutions. Furthermore, establishing clear communication channels and promoting transparent feedback mechanisms can help in enhancing the team's ability to adjust quickly to new challenges. Regular check-ins, status updates, and progress reports provide team members with the information they need to make informed decisions and adapt their strategies as needed.

It is also crucial to empower team members with the autonomy to make decisions within their domain, enabling them to respond promptly to changes without bureaucratic constraints. This sense of ownership fosters a proactive mindset and instills a sense of responsibility, key elements in cultivating a flexible team culture. Recognizing and celebrating instances where the team has demonstrated adaptability and resilience can reinforce these behaviors. By acknowledging and rewarding individuals and groups who have successfully navigated challenging situations, leaders can incentivize and inspire others to embrace flexibility and innovation.

Investing in continuous learning and development opportunities for the team can further nurture a flexible culture. Encouraging the acquisition of new skills, knowledge, and expertise enables team members to adapt to evolving demands and remain at the forefront of industry trends. Empowering the team with the tools they need to thrive in changing environments reaffirms the organization's commitment to adaptability and sets the stage for sustained success.

Strategies for Overcoming Adversity

Adversity is an inevitable part of professional life, and the ability to overcome it is a defining characteristic of successful individuals and organizations. *Firstly, acknowledging the adversity and understanding its root causes is crucial. By identifying the specific challenges, individuals can begin to formulate targeted solutions to address them. Next, harnessing a resilient mindset within the team can* significantly impact how adversity is confronted. Encouraging open communication and promoting a supportive environment can empower team members to face challenges with courage and determination.

Leveraging past successes as a source of motivation and inspiration can infuse optimism into the team during difficult times. Additionally, creating a contingency plan and building a strong support network can provide a safety net when navigating through uncertainty. It's important to foster a culture that embraces innovative thinking and risk-taking, allowing for creative problem-solving in the face of adversity.

Embracing change rather than resisting it can shift perspectives and lead to new opportunities amidst adversity. Finally, continuously evaluating and adapting strategies based on lessons learned from previous adversities can contribute to long-term resilience and success. By implementing these strategies, individuals and teams can proactively approach adversity, turning challenges into opportunities for growth and innovation.

Leveraging Failure as an Opportunity

It is often said that failure is a stepping stone to success. This holds especially true in the dynamic and competitive landscape of business. Instead of viewing failure as a setback, successful individuals and organizations understand its potential as a catalyst for growth and innovation. *When confronted with failure, it is crucial to adopt a growth mindset that embraces challenges as opportunities for learning and improvement.* By reframing failure in this manner, individuals can transform setbacks into valuable experiences that propel them forward. One approach to leveraging failure is through comprehensive post-mortems or debriefing sessions. These sessions allow teams to dissect the reasons behind the failure, identify key learnings, and form action plans for future success.

Encouraging open dialogue about failures within an organization fosters a culture of transparency and continuous improvement. This culture empowers employees to take calculated risks and learn from their mistakes, ultimately driving innovation and resilience. Another pivotal aspect of leveraging failure is the concept of 'failing fast.' In today's fast-paced business environment, the ability to quickly recognize and acknowledge failure is essential. This enables organizations to pivot, adapt, and iterate on their strategies without prolonging detrimental impacts. It also instills a sense of resilience, as team members become accustomed to navigating uncertainty and rebounding from setbacks. Furthermore, leaders play a crucial role in setting the tone for embracing failure as a growth opportunity.

By openly sharing their own experiences of overcoming failure and showcasing vulnerability, they demonstrate that setbacks are not indicative of incompetence, but rather integral components of success. This transparency fosters trust and encourages others to adopt a similar approach towards failure. Ultimately, by leveraging failure as a growth opportunity, individuals and organizations can harness adversity to fuel progress, foster resilience, and drive meaningful change.

Innovating Under Pressure

Amidst the turbulent winds of change, the ability to innovate under pressure sets apart visionary leaders from the masses. When organizations face unprecedented challenges or swiftly evolving market landscapes, the capacity to innovate becomes a critical lifeline for sustainable success. As external pressures mount, so too does the urgency to pivot, adapt, and create novel solutions that defy convention. *The greatest innovations often emerge during moments of intense pressure, when creativity is ignited by necessity.* In these high-stakes scenarios, leaders must foster an environment where unconventional thinking is not only encouraged but revered. By nurturing a culture of innovation, organizations can harness the collective ingenuity of their teams to overcome seemingly insurmountable obstacles.

Amidst adversity, forward-thinking leaders recognize that complacency is the enemy, and breakthroughs require resilience and audacious thinking. Strategic risk-taking becomes the crucible through which transformative ideas are forged. Identifying and capitalizing on emerging opportunities amidst chaos demands agility, courage, and unwavering determination. Beyond the cacophony of uncertainty, the beacon of innovation illuminates a path towards reinvention and renewal.

Sustainable growth in the face of adversity hinges on an organization's ability to relentlessly pursue new horizons, refusing to succumb to the status quo. Through swift, decisive action and a commitment to continuous improvement, leaders pave the way for sustainable adaptation in a volatile world. The journey of innovating under pressure is not without its challenges, but it breeds unyielding fortitude, clarity of purpose, and evolution. Thus, as turbulent tides surge, those who dare to innovate unflinchingly under pressure carve out a legacy of trailblazing resilience.

Sustaining Success Through Continuous Adaptation

As the business landscape continues to evolve at an unprecedented pace, sustaining success requires a proactive approach to continuous adaptation. Organizations must develop a culture that embraces change as a constant, leveraging it as a springboard for innovation and growth. Embracing adaptability as a core value empowers teams to anticipate and respond to market shifts, technological advancements, and consumer trends. *By building an environment where flexibility and agility are prized, companies can position themselves to thrive in the face of uncertainty.*

The process of continuous adaptation involves regularly reassessing strategies, processes, and structures to ensure they remain aligned with evolving external and internal factors. This ongoing introspection enables organizations to identify areas for improvement and swiftly implement necessary changes. The commitment to continuous adaptation broods a mindset of perpetual learning and improvement, driving organizational evolution and resilience. In essence, success is not determined by remaining static, but by embracing change as a catalyst for sustained relevance and competitiveness. By continuously adapting, businesses can stay ahead of the curve, anticipating shifts in the market and customer needs.

Adaptable organizations are better equipped to pivot quickly, minimize disruption, and capitalize on emerging opportunities. The synergy between adaptability and resilience enables companies to navigate challenges with grace, emerging stronger and more agile. Sustaining success through continuous adaptation necessitates a holistic approach that permeates every level of the organization, from leadership to front-line employees. It's a commitment to embracing change, fostering innovation, and cultivating resilience that truly distinguishes thriving enterprises in today's dynamic business landscape.

Strategies for Self-Improvement

Adaptability and resilience are essential qualities for thriving in today's fast-paced, ever-changing business environment. Challenges and their strategies for navigating through are presented below:

1. Coping with Change

Challenge: Managing and adapting to constant changes in the workplace, industry, and market conditions.

Self-Development Strategies:

Change Management Skills:

- *Training*: Enroll in change management courses to learn frameworks and strategies for managing change effectively.

- *Certification:* Consider certifications such as Prosci Change Management Certification to deepen your knowledge.

Flexibility:

- *Mindset*: Cultivate a growth mindset by embracing change as an opportunity for growth and learning.

- *Experimentation*: Practice flexibility by experimenting with new approaches and being open to feedback and adjustments.

Stress Management:

- *Mindfulness Practices*: Incorporate mindfulness practices such as deep breathing to manage stress and stay focused during change.

- *Physical Health*: Maintain good physical health through regular exercise, a balanced diet, and adequate sleep to build resilience against stress.

2. Overcoming Setbacks

Challenge: Bouncing back from failures and setbacks without losing motivation or confidence.

Self-Development Strategies:

Resilience Building:

- *Positive Psychology*: Study positive psychology principles to build a more optimistic and resilient mindset.

- *Resilience Training:* Participate in resilience training programs that focus on techniques for bouncing back from adversity.

Learning from Failure:

- *Reflection:* Develop a habit of reflecting on setbacks to identify lessons learned and areas for improvement.

- *Failure Analysis*: Conduct failure analysis to understand the root causes and implement changes to prevent recurrence.

3. Managing Uncertainty

Challenge: Navigating uncertainty and making decisions with incomplete information.

Self-Development Strategies:

Decision-Making Skills:

- *Decision Frameworks*: Learn and apply decision-making frameworks such as the OODA loop (Observe, Orient, Decide, Act) or the Cynefin framework.
- *Risk Management*: Study risk management techniques to assess and mitigate uncertainties effectively.

Scenario Planning:

- *Scenario Analysis*: Practice scenario analysis to anticipate possible future scenarios and develop contingency plans.
- *Flexibility:* Be prepared to pivot and adjust plans based on new information and changing circumstances.

Adaptability Exercises:

- *Adaptation Challenges*: Engage in activities that require adaptability, such as improvisational exercises or problem-solving games.

- *Continuous Learning:* Commit to lifelong learning to stay adaptable by continuously acquiring new skills and knowledge.

4. Balancing Multiple Priorities

Challenge: Juggling multiple responsibilities and adapting to shifting priorities without becoming overwhelmed.

Self-Development Strategies:

Time Management:

- *Prioritization Techniques*: Use prioritization techniques like the Eisenhower Matrix to focus on tasks that are both urgent and important.

- *Time Blocking:* Implement time-blocking methods to allocate dedicated time slots for high-priority tasks.

Work-Life Balance:

- *Boundaries:* Set clear boundaries between work and personal life to prevent burnout and maintain overall well-being.

- *Downtime:* Schedule regular downtime and relaxation periods to recharge and maintain productivity.

Delegation:

- *Empower Others*: Delegate tasks to team members to manage workload effectively and focus on strategic priorities.

- *Trust Building:* Build trust with your team by providing clear instructions and support while allowing autonomy.

5. Maintaining Positive Relationships

Challenge: Building and maintaining positive relationships with colleagues, even under stressful or changing conditions.

Self-Development Strategies:

Emotional Intelligence:

- *EI Training*: Enhance your emotional intelligence (EI) through training and practice. Focus on self-awareness, self-regulation, empathy, and social skills.

- *Empathy Exercises*: Engage in empathy-building exercises to better understand and respond to others' emotions and perspectives.

Conflict Resolution:

- *Conflict Management Skills*: Learn conflict management techniques to address and resolve conflicts constructively.
- *Active Listening*: Practice active listening to understand others' viewpoints and foster open communication.

Networking:

- *Relationship Building*: Invest time in building and nurturing relationships with colleagues and industry peers.
- *Collaboration:* Promote collaboration and teamwork by creating opportunities for team-building activities and collaborative projects.

9

CUSTOMER FOCUS

"Customer focus is not just a business strategy; it is a philosophy of understanding and anticipating the needs and desires of those we serve. In prioritizing the customer, we not only drive success but also cultivate trust and loyalty that form the essence of enduring relationships."

Understanding Customer Needs

Understanding customer needs is crucial for any business striving to achieve sustainable success. Various methods can be employed to identify what customers truly desire, with market research and direct feedback standing out as essential tools in this quest. Market research involves the systematic gathering, recording, and analysis of data pertaining to customers' behavior, preferences, and purchasing patterns. This can be achieved through surveys, focus groups, and data analytics, providing valuable insights into consumer trends and demands.

Direct feedback from customers themselves provides firsthand information about their experiences, challenges, and expectations. Whether obtained through customer service interactions, online reviews, or social media engagement, this feedback serves as a goldmine of actionable intelligence. By actively listening to their concerns and suggestions, businesses can gain a profound understanding of their customers' needs. Engaging in dialogue with customers fosters trust and demonstrates a commitment to meeting their needs.

Recognizing that customer needs are dynamic and constantly evolving is essential. Businesses must remain agile, continuously adapting to changing preferences and requirements to ensure that their offerings remain relevant and compelling. By proactively seeking to understand and cater to customer needs, businesses can foster loyalty, drive innovation, and ultimately thrive in today's competitive marketplace.

Building Strong Relationships

Building strong relationships with customers is crucial for long-term success in any business. It goes beyond providing a product or service; it involves creating trust, loyalty, and a sense of partnership. The foundation of a strong relationship lies in understanding the customer's needs, goals, and challenges. *By actively listening to their concerns and feedback, businesses can demonstrate empathy and commitment to solving their problems.* This genuine interest in their well-being fosters a deeper connection and builds trust. Consistency is also key in relationship-building. Providing consistent, high-quality service and delivering on promises reinforces reliability and stability.

Customers need to feel confident in the reliability and predictability of their interactions with a company. Transparency and open communication are vital components of strong relationships. Sharing information about products, services, and company developments helps create a sense of inclusion and involvement. It also allows customers to make informed decisions, thereby empowering them in their interactions with the business. Acknowledging and expressing appreciation for customers is essential in building strong relationships. Recognizing their loyalty and offering personalized gestures, such as thank-you notes or exclusive offers, can strengthen emotional connections.

Resolving issues and conflicts promptly and effectively is crucial in maintaining a positive relationship. How a business handles mistakes or setbacks can significantly impact the customer's perception and loyalty. By demonstrating accountability and a commitment to making things right, businesses can turn negative experiences into opportunities for strengthening the relationship. Building strong relationships isn't only about the present; it requires consideration of the future. Anticipating and adapting to evolving customer needs and trends is essential for staying relevant and meeting expectations. By being proactive and forward-thinking, businesses can demonstrate their dedication to serving customers' changing requirements. Ultimately, a focus on building strong relationships cultivates customer loyalty, advocacy, and a positive reputation. It positions businesses for sustained success and growth by fostering meaningful, mutually beneficial connections.

Personalizing Customer Interactions

To truly excel in customer focus, businesses need to go beyond the traditional approach of treating all customers the same. Personalizing customer interactions involves understanding the unique preferences, behaviors, and needs of individual customers and tailoring the service or product offerings accordingly. This level of personalization can significantly enhance the overall customer experience and build stronger loyalty.

Personalization starts with data collection and analysis. By gathering information about customers' past purchases, browsing behavior, demographics, and feedback, businesses can gain valuable insights into what each customer values. Utilizing advanced analytics and artificial intelligence, companies can segment their customer base and create personalized recommendations, offers, and communication strategies for different segments.

Personalizing customer interactions extends beyond marketing and sales efforts. It also encompasses the customer support experience. Imagine a scenario where a customer contacts support, and the representative already knows who they are, understands their past issues, and can provide tailored assistance based on the customer's history with the company. This level of personalization not only resolves issues more efficiently but also enhances the customer's perception of the brand.

In addition to leveraging data and technology, personalizing customer interactions requires a human touch. It involves training and empowering employees to engage with customers on a personal level, listening attentively to their concerns, and offering genuine, empathetic assistance. *Customers appreciate feeling understood and valued as individuals, and personalization can help create this emotional connection.*

Another crucial aspect of personalizing customer interactions is creating *seamless omnichannel experiences.* Customers expect consistency and continuity across various touchpoints, whether it's the company's website, social media channels, mobile apps, or in-person interactions. By integrating these channels and ensuring that customer data and preferences are accessible across all touchpoints, businesses can create cohesive and personalized experiences that resonate with customers.

Personalization should be an ongoing process, continuously adapting to evolving customer needs and market trends. By seeking regular feedback and actively listening to customers, businesses can refine their personalization strategies to stay relevant and meet changing expectations. The ability to personalize customer interactions effectively is a hallmark of customer-focused organizations, setting them apart in a highly competitive landscape.

Implementing Customer Feedback

As businesses strive to maintain a strong customer focus, implementing customer feedback becomes an integral aspect of their operations. *Customer feedback offers invaluable insights into the performance of products, services, and overall customer experience.* By actively seeking and incorporating customer feedback, organizations can identify areas for improvement and make informed decisions to enhance their offerings. One of the most effective ways to implement customer feedback is through *systematic data collection and analysis.* This involves gathering feedback from various touchpoints such as surveys, social media, direct interactions, and online reviews. Once the feedback is collected, it should be carefully analyzed to identify recurring patterns, emerging trends, and key pain points. Organizations can then categorize and prioritize feedback based on its significance and impact. Implementing customer feedback also requires a commitment to action. It's not enough to simply collect and analyze feedback; organizations must demonstrate a willingness to act on the insights gained. This may involve making changes to products or services, revising internal processes, or refining customer interactions. Additionally, communicating the actions taken in response to customer feedback can help build trust and show customers that their input is valued.

Organizations should establish clear accountability for implementing customer feedback. Designating specific teams or individuals to oversee the implementation process can ensure that feedback is systematically addressed and integrated into the organization's strategic objectives. An essential aspect of implementing customer feedback is building a culture of continuous improvement. Organizations should view customer feedback as an ongoing source of learning and development, rather than a one-time activity. This mindset encourages proactive adaptation and innovation, driving the organization towards sustained excellence in meeting customer needs and expectations. Implementing customer feedback is a dynamic and iterative process that requires dedicated effort and a customer-centric mindset. By leveraging the valuable insights gleaned from customer feedback, organizations can stay attuned to evolving customer preferences, refine their offerings, and build long-lasting relationships with their clientele.

Leveraging Technology for Better Service

Leveraging the latest technological advancements is imperative for businesses to provide better service to their customers. With the advent of artificial intelligence, machine learning, chatbots, and data analytics, businesses can now harness the power of technology to enhance their customer service. One of the key ways technology improves service is through automation. Automated systems can handle routine tasks, such as answering frequently asked questions, processing orders, and providing basic product information, allowing human employees to focus on more complex issues and personalized interactions with customers.

Technology enables businesses to provide omnichannel support, allowing customers to engage across multiple platforms seamlessly. This means that customers can reach out for support via phone, email, chat, social media, or in-person, and still receive consistent and reliable assistance. The use of customer relationship management (CRM) software discussed earlier, enables businesses to access valuable customer data and interactions, leading to a better understanding of individual needs and preferences. This data-driven approach allows for highly personalized and targeted service, ultimately leading to higher levels of customer satisfaction and loyalty.

Proactive technology, such as predictive analytics, empowers businesses to anticipate customer needs and provide preemptive support, thereby enhancing the overall customer experience. By integrating technology into their service strategies, businesses can achieve greater efficiency, accuracy, and speed in addressing customer needs. However, it's essential to maintain a balance between technology and the human touch. While technology can streamline and optimize processes, human empathy and emotional intelligence are irreplaceable when it comes to providing truly exceptional service. Therefore, businesses must ensure that technology complements, rather than replaces, the human element in customer interactions. In sum, leveraging technology for better service involves embracing automation, utilizing omnichannel support, harnessing data-driven insights, and maintaining a delicate balance between technology and human interaction. When implemented thoughtfully, technology can elevate the quality of customer service, ultimately contributing to long-term business success and customer satisfaction.

Empathy and Emotional Intelligence

Empathy and emotional intelligence are critical components of providing exceptional customer service. *Empathy involves the ability to understand and share the feelings of another person.* When interacting with customers, it is essential to empathize with their concerns, challenges, and emotions. By putting yourself in the customer's shoes, you can gain a deeper understanding of their perspective and tailor your approach to meet their needs effectively.

Emotional intelligence, on the other hand, encompasses the capacity to recognize, understand, and manage emotions, both within oneself and in others. In a customer service context, this means being aware of your own emotions and reactions, as well as accurately interpreting and responding to the emotions of customers. Developing emotional intelligence allows you to build rapport with customers, defuse tense situations, and foster positive interactions. To enhance empathy and emotional intelligence in customer interactions, it is crucial to actively listen to customers, demonstrate genuine concern for their experiences, and show understanding and compassion.

Utilizing non-verbal cues, such as body language and tone of voice, can convey empathy and help create a connection with the customer. Training programs focusing on emotional intelligence and empathy can be beneficial for customer service representatives, as they provide practical tools and techniques for effectively managing challenging interactions. Building a work culture that values empathy and emotional intelligence promotes a customer-centric approach throughout an organization. By prioritizing these qualities in customer service, businesses can build stronger relationships with customers, increase satisfaction, and differentiate themselves in the market. Displaying empathy and emotional intelligence towards customers not only drives loyalty and retention but also contributes to the overall success of a business.

Measuring Customer Satisfaction

Measuring customer satisfaction is essential for any business looking to succeed in today's competitive market. It provides valuable insights into how well the company is meeting customer expectations and where improvements may be needed. There are various methods for measuring customer satisfaction, including *surveys, direct feedback, and net promoter scores.* Surveys can be conducted online, via email, or through in-person interviews to gauge overall satisfaction with products, services, and overall experience with the brand. Direct feedback, whether through customer service interactions or online reviews, offers immediate insight into specific pain points or areas of delight for customers. Net promoter scores assess customer loyalty by asking how likely customers are to recommend the company to others. By analyzing these metrics, businesses can identify areas for improvement and leverage strengths to enhance overall customer satisfaction. It allows businesses to track changes in customer sentiment over time, providing a benchmark for performance and progress. Effective measurement of customer satisfaction should not only focus on quantitative data but also consider qualitative feedback. Understanding the *'why'* behind customer perceptions and sentiments is crucial for making meaningful improvements. This could involve engaging in deep-dive discussions with select customers or conducting focus groups to gain deeper insights.

Leveraging technology such as *sentiment analysis tools and social media monitoring* can provide real-time feedback and sentiment analysis, enabling proactive response to potential issues and capitalizing on positive moments. Measuring customer satisfaction is critical for maintaining a customer-centric approach and sustaining long-term success. When done effectively, it enables businesses to make data-driven decisions, prioritize initiatives that directly impact customer experience, and ultimately drive growth and loyalty.

Resolving Conflicts Effectively

Conflicts in a business setting are inevitable, and how they are managed can significantly impact customer satisfaction and retention.

Resolving conflicts effectively requires a combination of communication, empathy, and problem-solving skills. When a conflict arises, it's essential to address it promptly and with sensitivity. Active listening is a crucial component of conflict resolution as it allows for a better understanding of the issue at hand. Both parties should be given the opportunity to express their perspectives without interruption. Once each side has had the chance to communicate their viewpoints, the next step is finding common ground and seeking a mutually beneficial solution. This could involve brainstorming alternative options or compromises. It's important to acknowledge the emotions involved in the conflict and show empathy towards the affected parties. Empathy helps in building rapport and trust, which is essential for conflict resolution. Conflict resolution also involves understanding the root cause of the conflict.

Sometimes, conflicts surface due to *misunderstandings, differing expectations, or even external factors beyond the control of either party.* Identifying the underlying causes can provide clarity and facilitate the resolution process. Having a clear and documented process for addressing conflicts can streamline the resolution process. This includes defining roles and responsibilities in conflict resolution, establishing escalation procedures, and ensuring that resolutions are implemented effectively. *Conflicts can be an opportunity for improvement.* By analyzing past conflicts and their resolutions, businesses can identify recurring issues and work towards preventing similar conflicts in the future. It's important to follow up after the conflict has been resolved to ensure that the solution is effective and satisfactory for all involved parties. By implementing these strategies for resolving conflicts effectively, businesses can not only enhance customer satisfaction but also create a positive and inclusive work environment.

Handling Customer Complaints

Effectively handling customer complaints is crucial for maintaining customer satisfaction and loyalty. How you respond to complaints can turn a negative experience into a positive one and demonstrate your commitment to customer service. Here we will explore strategies for addressing and resolving customer complaints.

1. Active Listening:

Empathetic Listening: Listen to the customer's complaint with empathy and understanding. Show genuine concern for their issue and acknowledge their feelings.

Clarifying Questions: Ask clarifying questions to fully understand the problem. Ensure that you have all the necessary details to address the complaint effectively.

2. Prompt Response:

Timely Acknowledgment: Acknowledge the complaint promptly, even if you don't have an immediate solution. Let the customer know that their concern is being taken seriously.

Swift Resolution: Aim to resolve the complaint as quickly as possible. Timely solutions demonstrate efficiency and respect for the customer's time.

3. Apologizing and Taking Responsibility:

Sincere Apology: Offer a sincere apology for any inconvenience caused. Acknowledging the mistake can help diffuse tension and show that you value the customer's experience.

Taking Responsibility: Take full responsibility for the issue, even if it was beyond your control. Avoid shifting blame and focus on finding a resolution.

4. Providing Solutions:

Proactive Solutions: Offer practical and fair solutions to the customer's problem. Ensure that the resolution addresses their concerns and restores their satisfaction.

Alternative Options: If a single solution isn't feasible, provide alternative options. Giving customers a choice can make them feel more in control of the situation.

5. Follow-Up:

Confirming Resolution: Follow up with the customer after resolving the complaint to ensure they are satisfied with the outcome. This extra step shows that you care about their continued satisfaction.

Gathering Feedback: Ask for feedback on how the complaint was handled. Use this information to improve your complaint-handling processes and prevent future issues.

6. Learning from Complaints:

Root Cause Analysis: Analyze the root cause of recurring complaints to identify underlying issues. Addressing these root causes can prevent similar problems in the future.

Continuous Improvement: Use customer complaints as opportunities for continuous improvement. Implement changes based on feedback to enhance overall customer satisfaction.

7. Training and Empowering Staff:

Customer Service Training: Train your staff to handle complaints effectively and empathetically. Equip them with the skills and knowledge needed to resolve issues efficiently.

Empowerment: Empower your staff to make decisions and take actions to resolve complaints. Giving them the authority to act can lead to faster and more effective resolutions.

8. Creating a Positive Experience:

Turning Negatives into Positives: Aim to turn negative experiences into positive ones by exceeding the customer's expectations in the resolution process. Going the extra mile can leave a lasting positive impression.

Personal Touch: Add a personal touch to the resolution process, such as a handwritten apology note or a follow-up call. Personal gestures can significantly enhance customer satisfaction.

9. Maintaining Transparency:

Honest Communication: Be honest and transparent throughout the complaint resolution process. Keep the customer informed about what is being done to address their issue.

Setting Expectations: Clearly set expectations regarding the timeline for resolution and any actions being taken. Managing expectations helps prevent further frustration.

10. Building a Feedback Loop:

Systematic Feedback Collection: Implement systems for systematically collecting and analyzing customer complaints. Use this data to identify trends and areas for improvement.

Acting on Feedback: Demonstrate that you value customer feedback by making tangible improvements based on their input. Showing that you act on feedback reinforces customer trust and loyalty.

Creating a Customer-Centric Culture

A customer-centric culture requires a company-wide commitment to prioritizing the needs and experiences of customers in every aspect of the business. It involves aligning the organization's values, operations, and goals with the goal of delivering exceptional customer satisfaction. To create a customer-centric culture, leadership must not only advocate for customer-centricity but also embody it in their actions and decisions. This involves setting an example for employees by consistently prioritizing customer needs and feedback.

Companies must empower their employees to make decisions that prioritize the customer, creating a sense of ownership and accountability. Communication is paramount in establishing a customer-centric culture. Clear and consistent communication channels facilitate the understanding and dissemination of customer feedback and insights across all levels of the organization. Cultivating empathy among employees is crucial in building a customer-centric culture. Employees who can deeply understand and address customer needs are better equipped to deliver personalized solutions and experiences. In addition to empathy, a focus on *continuous improvement* is fundamental in creating a customer-centric culture. Companies must continuously evaluate and adapt their processes, products, and services to better serve their customers. Recognizing and rewarding employees who exemplify outstanding customer-centric behavior reinforces the importance of this culture within the organization. A customer-centric culture not only leads to increased customer loyalty and satisfaction but also drives innovation and growth. As businesses evolve, embracing and embedding a customer-centric philosophy throughout the organization will be a key differentiator in maintaining a competitive edge.

Building Customer Loyalty

Customer loyalty is essential for long-term business success. Loyal customers not only provide repeat business but also act as brand advocates, attracting new customers through word-of-mouth and firsthand experience.

1. Offering Exceptional Customer Service:

Consistent Quality: Ensure that your products or services consistently meet or exceed customer expectations. Quality and reliability are key factors in retaining customers.

Personalized Experiences: Personalize interactions and tailor your services to meet individual customer needs. Use customer data to understand preferences and offer customized solutions.

2. Building Strong Relationships:

Regular Communication: Keep in touch with your customers through regular updates, newsletters, and personalized messages. Consistent communication helps maintain a connection and keeps your brand top of mind.

Engagement: Engage with customers through social media, surveys, and events. Actively listening to their feedback and involving them in your brand's community fosters a sense of belonging.

3. Rewarding Loyalty:

Loyalty Programs: Implement loyalty programs that reward repeat customers with discounts, special offers, or exclusive access to new products. Such programs incentivize continued patronage.

Referral Programs: Encourage loyal customers to refer new clients by offering rewards for successful referrals. This not only brings in new business but also strengthens the relationship with existing customers.

4. Providing Excellent After-Sales Support:

Customer Support: Offer robust after-sales support to assist customers with any issues or questions. Prompt and helpful responses build trust and reinforce loyalty.

Follow-Up: Follow up with customers after a purchase to ensure satisfaction and gather feedback. Showing that you care about their experience even after the sale strengthens their loyalty.

5. Building Trust and Transparency:

Honesty: Be transparent and honest in all your dealings with customers. Trust is a foundational element of customer loyalty.

Integrity: Admit and rectify mistakes promptly. Demonstrating integrity when things go wrong can turn a negative experience into a positive one.

6. Creating Value:

Educational Content: Provide valuable content that helps customers get the most out of your products or services. Educational resources, tutorials, and webinars can enhance their experience.

Continuous Improvement: Continuously improve your offerings based on customer feedback and market trends. Showing that you are committed to adding value over time reinforces loyalty.

7. Emotional Connection:

Brand Storytelling: Share your brand's story and values in a way that resonates with your customers. Emotional connections can strengthen loyalty and make your brand more memorable.

Human Touch: Humanize your brand by showcasing the people behind it. Personal stories and interactions create a deeper connection with customers.

8. Consistent Branding:

Unified Experience: Ensure that all customer touchpoints provide a consistent brand experience. Consistency in messaging, visuals, and tone reinforces brand identity and loyalty.

Customer-Centric Culture: Foster a customer-centric culture within your organization. Employees who are committed to customer satisfaction contribute significantly to building loyalty.

9. Monitoring and Measuring Loyalty:

Customer Feedback: Regularly gather and analyze customer feedback to understand their needs and satisfaction levels. Use surveys, reviews, and direct feedback to gauge loyalty.

Net Promoter Score (NPS): Measure customer loyalty using the Net Promoter Score (NPS). This metric helps identify loyal customers and areas for improvement.

10. Adapting to Customer Needs:

Flexibility: Be flexible and responsive to changing customer needs and preferences. Adapting your products, services, and approaches based on customer input shows that you value their opinions.

Future Trends in Customer Service

The future of customer service is poised to be shaped by several key trends that are revolutionizing the way businesses interact with their customers. One of the most significant developments is the integration of *artificial intelligence (AI) and machine learning* in customer service processes. *AI-powered chatbots and virtual assistants* are becoming increasingly sophisticated, enabling businesses to provide personalized and efficient support round the clock. These advancements not only enhance customer satisfaction but also streamline internal operations. Another pivotal trend is the growing emphasis on omni-channel customer service. With the proliferation of communication channels such as social media, messaging apps, and virtual assistants, customers now expect seamless and consistent experiences across all platforms.

Businesses that can effectively integrate and manage these diverse channels will gain a competitive edge in the market. The evolution of self-service options is reshaping the customer service landscape. From interactive FAQs to automated troubleshooting tools, customers are increasingly turning to self-service solutions for quick resolutions. As technology continues to advance, so too will the range and capabilities of self-service offerings. The rise of proactive customer service is redefining traditional reactive support models. By leveraging data analytics and predictive algorithms, businesses can anticipate customer needs and provide preemptive assistance. This shift towards proactive engagement not only fosters stronger customer relationships but also mitigates potential issues before they escalate.

Ethical considerations in customer service are gaining prominence. Customers are increasingly mindful of data privacy and ethical business practices, prompting businesses to prioritize transparency and accountability in their interactions. Meeting these expectations will be imperative for building trust and loyalty in the evolving customer landscape. The *human touch* remains irreplaceable in customer service. While technology continues to innovate, the value of authentic human connections and empathetic communication cannot be overlooked. The future of customer service will demand a harmonious blend of technological prowess and human warmth to deliver exceptional experiences. As these trends continue to unfold, businesses must adapt and evolve to stay ahead in catering to the ever-changing needs and expectations of their customers.

Strategies for Self-Improvement

Customer focus is crucial for building strong relationships and ensuring business success. Here are the top five customer focus challenges and strategies for becoming a problem solver through self-development and improvement:

1. Understanding Customer Needs

Challenge: Gaining deep insights into customer needs, preferences, and pain points.

Self-Development Strategies:

Customer Research Skills:

- *Market Research Training:* Enroll in courses that teach market research techniques, including surveys, focus groups, and interviews.
- *Customer Journey Mapping:* Learn to create customer journey maps to visualize and understand the customer experience from start to finish.

Empathy and Active Listening:

- *Empathy Training:* Engage in empathy-building exercises to better understand and relate to customers' feelings and perspectives.

- *Active Listening*: Practice active listening techniques to fully capture and comprehend customer feedback.

Data Analysis:

- *Analytics Tools:* Learn to use customer analytics tools such as Google Analytics, CRM software, and social media monitoring tools to gather and analyze customer data.

- *Segmentation*: Study customer segmentation methods to categorize customers based on their behaviors and preferences.

2. Delivering Consistent Customer Experience

Challenge: Ensuring that customers have a consistent and positive experience across all touchpoints.

Self-Development Strategies:

Process Improvement:

- *Lean Six Sigma*: Take Lean Six Sigma courses to learn process improvement techniques that can enhance customer experience.

- *Service Design*: Study service design principles to create seamless and efficient customer interactions.

Customer Service Skills:

- *Customer Service Training*: Attend training sessions focused on developing exceptional customer service skills, including communication, problem-solving, and conflict resolution.

- *Customer Experience Management*: Learn customer experience management strategies to ensure consistency across all customer interactions.

Quality Assurance:

- *Standards and Protocols*: Develop and implement standards and protocols to ensure consistency in customer service delivery.

- *Regular Audits*: Conduct regular audits of customer interactions to identify areas for improvement and ensure adherence to standards.

3. Handling Customer Complaints and Feedback

Challenge: Effectively addressing customer complaints and leveraging feedback to improve products and services.

Self-Development Strategies:

Conflict Resolution:

- *Conflict Management Training*: Take courses in conflict management to develop skills in resolving customer complaints effectively.

- *De-escalation Techniques*: Learn de-escalation techniques to handle difficult customer interactions calmly and professionally.

Feedback Systems:

- *Survey Design*: Learn to design effective customer feedback surveys that gather actionable insights.

- *Feedback Analysis:* Study methods for analyzing feedback to identify trends and areas for improvement.

Continuous Improvement:

- *Kaizen*: Adopt the Kaizen philosophy of continuous improvement to regularly implement small, incremental changes based on customer feedback.

- *Root Cause Analysis*: Practice root cause analysis to identify and address the underlying causes of customer complaints.

4. Building Strong Customer Relationships

Challenge: Developing and maintaining long-term relationships with customers.

Self-Development Strategies:

Relationship Management:

- *CRM Tools*: Get trained in using CRM tools to manage and nurture customer relationships effectively.

- *Personalization*: Learn personalization techniques to tailor interactions and offers to individual customer needs.

Communication Skills:

- *Effective Communication*: Enhance your communication skills through courses and practice. Focus on clarity, empathy, and responsiveness.

- *Storytelling*: Learn storytelling techniques to engage customers and build a connection with your brand.

Trust Building:

- *Consistency and Reliability*: Develop a reputation for reliability by consistently delivering on promises and maintaining high standards.

- *Transparency:* Practice transparency in all customer interactions to build trust and credibility.

5. Aligning the Organization Around Customer Focus

Challenge: Ensuring that all departments and employees are aligned with a customer-centric approach.

Self-Development Strategies:

Leadership and Advocacy:

- *Customer Advocacy*: Take on the role of a customer advocate within your organization, promoting the importance of customer focus at all levels.

- *Leadership Training*: Attend leadership training programs that emphasize the importance of customer-centricity.

Cross-Functional Collaboration:

- *Team Building*: Foster cross-functional collaboration by organizing team-building activities and joint projects focused on improving customer experience.

- *Internal Communication*: Improve internal communication to ensure that customer feedback and insights are shared across departments.

Employee Training and Empowerment:

- *Customer-Centric Training*: Develop and deliver training programs that instill a customer-centric mindset in all employees.

- *Empowerment:* Empower employees to make decisions that benefit the customer, providing them with the tools and authority they need to act in the customer's best interest.

10

CONTINUOUS LEARNING AND DEVELOPMENT

"Continuous learning and development form the bedrock of personal and professional growth. Embrace the ceaseless journey of knowledge, not merely to remain relevant, but to transcend and evolve into your fullest potential."

The Imperative for Continuous Learning

Advancements in technology, shifts in consumer behaviors, and changing market dynamics necessitate that professionals consistently adapt to these developments to remain relevant and competitive. Industry trends are constantly in flux, and the ability to stay abreast of these changes is essential for both personal and organizational growth. *Embracing a culture of continuous learning not only helps individuals refine their skill sets but also enables organizations to maintain their edge in an increasingly competitive environment.* The potential consequences of failing to adapt can be severe; outdated skills and knowledge can render employees obsolete and businesses uncompetitive. Therefore, understanding and acknowledging the significance of continuous learning is crucial for sustained success in today's business world.

Professional Development Opportunities

Investing in professional development is crucial for personal growth and career advancement. By continually enhancing your skills and knowledge, you can stay competitive and effective in your field.

Opportunities and strategies for professional development.

1. Formal Education:

Advanced Degrees: Pursue advanced degrees such as a Master's or Doctorate to deepen your expertise and open up new career opportunities.

Certification Programs: Obtain certifications relevant to your field to demonstrate specialized knowledge and skills. Certifications can enhance your credibility and marketability.

2. Workshops and Seminars:

Industry Workshops: Attend workshops and seminars to gain practical skills and knowledge. These events often provide hands-on experience and networking opportunities.

Professional Conferences: Participate in professional conferences to stay updated on the latest trends and innovations in your industry. Conferences also offer opportunities to connect with thought leaders and peers.

3. Online Courses and Webinars:

E-Learning Platforms: Utilize e-learning platforms like Coursera, Udemy, and LinkedIn Learning to access a wide range of courses on various topics. Online courses offer flexibility and convenience.

Live Webinars: Attend live webinars hosted by industry experts to gain insights and engage in real-time discussions. Webinars often cover current trends and practical tips.

4. Mentorship and Coaching:

Finding a Mentor: Seek out mentors who can provide guidance, advice, and support based on their experience and expertise. Mentorship relationships can accelerate your professional growth.

Professional Coaching: Consider working with a professional coach to develop specific skills, set career goals, and overcome challenges. Coaching can provide personalized support and accountability.

5. Professional Associations:

Joining Associations: Become a member of professional associations related to your field. Associations offer resources, networking opportunities, and access to industry publications.

Active Participation: Participate actively in association events, committees, and leadership roles. Active involvement can enhance your professional reputation and provide valuable experience.

6. On-the-Job Training:

Cross-Training: Engage in cross-training to learn different roles and functions within your organization. Cross-training broadens your skill set and increases your versatility.

Job Rotations: Explore job rotation programs to gain exposure to various departments and functions. Rotations can provide a holistic understanding of the organization and enhance your career prospects.

7. Reading and Research:

Industry Publications: Subscribe to industry journals, magazines, and newsletters to stay informed about the latest developments and trends.

Books and Articles: Read books and articles written by experts in your field. Continuous reading broadens your knowledge and provides new perspectives.

8. Networking:

Professional Networking: Build and maintain a professional network through events, social media, and professional associations. Networking can lead to new opportunities and valuable collaborations.

Peer Groups: Join peer groups or mastermind groups to share knowledge, discuss challenges, and learn from others in similar roles.

9. Skill Development Programs:

Technical Skills: Enroll in programs that enhance technical skills relevant to your role, such as coding, data analysis, or project management.

Soft Skills: Develop soft skills such as communication, leadership, and emotional intelligence through targeted training programs.

10. Personal Development:

Work-Life Balance: Invest in personal development activities that promote work-life balance and well-being. Personal development contributes to overall effectiveness and satisfaction.

Lifelong Learning: Embrace a mindset of lifelong learning. Continuously seek opportunities to learn and grow, both personally and professionally.

Personal and Corporate Learning Needs

To develop a culture of continuous learning and development, it is crucial to conduct a comprehensive assessment of both personal and organizational learning needs. This assessment serves as the foundation for designing effective learning programs that align with the specific requirements of individuals and the overall strategic goals of the organization.

Assessing personal learning needs begins with understanding the skills, knowledge, and competencies required for each role within the organization. This involves conducting individual skill assessments, performance reviews, and feedback sessions to identify areas for improvement and growth. Employees can be encouraged to self-assess their strengths and weaknesses, providing valuable insights into their own developmental needs.

Understanding organizational learning needs entails, a thorough analysis of the current and future skill gaps, industry trends, technological advancements, and competitive landscape. By leveraging tools such as surveys, interviews, and data analytics, organizations can gain a holistic understanding of the learning requirements across various departments and levels of the workforce.

It is essential to involve key stakeholders in the assessment process, including leaders, managers, and subject matter experts. Their perspectives and inputs are invaluable in identifying challenges, opportunities, and the overarching learning priorities that will drive organizational success.

A proactive approach to identify learning needs also involves staying abreast of market disruptions, customer demands, and industry shifts. This foresight allows organizations to anticipate future skills requirements and preemptively address potential gaps, thus ensuring readiness for upcoming changes.

By diligently assessing personal and organizational learning needs, organizations can tailor their learning and development initiatives to directly address the identified gaps and propel individuals and the company towards achieving peak performance and excellence.

Staying Ahead of Industry Trends

Keeping up with industry trends is essential for maintaining a competitive edge and adapting to changes in your field. By staying informed about the latest developments, you can anticipate challenges, seize opportunities, and innovate effectively.

The strategies for staying ahead of industry trends.

1. Market Research:

Trend Analysis: Regularly conduct market research to identify emerging trends and shifts in your industry. Analyze data from various sources to gain insights into market dynamics.

Competitor Analysis: Monitor competitors to understand their strategies, strengths, and weaknesses. Competitor analysis helps you identify industry standards and innovation opportunities.

2. Industry Publications and Reports:

Subscribe to Reports: Subscribe to industry reports, whitepapers, and market analysis from reputable sources. These publications provide in-depth insights into current trends and future projections.

Trade Magazines: Read trade magazines and industry journals to stay updated on news, innovations, and best practices.

3. Networking and Professional Associations:

Industry Events: Attend industry conferences, trade shows, and networking events to learn about the latest trends and connect with experts.

Association Memberships: Join professional associations to access exclusive resources, research, and events that highlight industry trends.

4. Online Resources:

Websites and Blogs: Follow industry websites, blogs, and influencers to get timely updates on trends and innovations.

Social Media: Use social media platforms like LinkedIn, X, and industry-specific forums to engage in discussions and stay informed about current developments.

5. Continuous Learning:

Online Courses: Enroll in online courses that focus on emerging trends and new technologies. E-learning platforms offer courses on a wide range of topics.

Workshops and Seminars: Participate in workshops and seminars that explore the latest trends and innovations. These events provide hands-on learning and networking opportunities.

6. Collaboration and Partnerships:

Collaborate with Innovators: Partner with innovative companies, startups, and research institutions to gain insights into cutting-edge developments.

Industry Projects: Engage in industry projects and consortiums that focus on research and innovation. Collaboration can lead to valuable insights and advancements.

7. Thought Leadership:

Publishing and Speaking: Share your expertise through publishing articles, authoring books, whitepapers, and speaking at conferences. Thought leadership positions you as an authority in your field and keeps you engaged with current trends.

Panel Discussions: Participate in panel discussions and roundtables to exchange ideas with other experts and gain diverse perspectives.

8. Technology Adoption:

Embrace New Technologies: Stay open to adopting new technologies that can improve efficiency, productivity, and innovation. Experiment with tools and platforms that offer competitive advantages.

Technology Training: Provide training for yourself and your team on new technologies and their applications. Staying proficient with the latest tools is essential for staying ahead.

9. Customer Feedback:

Customer Insights: Gather feedback from customers to understand their evolving needs and preferences. Customer insights can reveal trends and guide product development.

Market Testing: Conduct market testing and pilot programs to assess the viability of new ideas and innovations. Real-world feedback helps validate trends and guide strategic decisions.

10. Scenario Planning:

Future Scenarios: Develop and analyze future scenarios to anticipate potential changes in your industry. Scenario planning helps you prepare for various outcomes and adapt strategies accordingly.

Strategic Foresight: Utilize strategic foresight techniques to identify and evaluate emerging trends. This proactive approach enables you to stay ahead of the curve and make informed decisions.

By actively pursuing professional development opportunities and staying ahead of industry trends, you can enhance your skills, remain competitive, and drive innovation in your field.

Modern Learning Techniques and Tools

The demand for continuous learning has never been greater. With the rapid advancement of technology and the ever-evolving global landscape, individuals and organizations are constantly seeking modern learning techniques and tools to stay ahead of the curve. Modern learning has transcended traditional methods, embracing a range of innovative approaches and cutting-edge tools that cater to diverse learning styles and preferences.

One of the most prominent modern learning techniques is **e-learning**, which offers the flexibility and convenience of accessing educational resources from anywhere at any time. E-learning encompasses various formats, including interactive online courses, webinars, virtual classrooms, and educational videos. These platforms provide learners with the freedom to personalize their learning experience and progress at their own pace, making education more accessible and inclusive.

Gamification has emerged as a powerful tool for enhancing engagement and retention in learning. By incorporating elements of game design, such as challenges, rewards, and competition, into educational content, gamification motivates learners and makes the learning process inherently enjoyable. This approach breeds a competitive spirit and encourages active participation, leading to improved knowledge retention and application.

Another modern technique gaining traction is *microlearning,* which involves delivering educational content in bite-sized segments. *Microlearning is particularly effective in catering to the decreasing attention spans of modern learners, as it provides succinct and focused information that can be easily consumed and retained.* Through short modules, videos, or quizzes, microlearning allows learners to quickly acquire specific skills or knowledge in a time-efficient manner.

The proliferation of virtual reality (VR) and augmented reality (AR) technologies has revolutionized immersive learning experiences. These technologies enable learners to engage in realistic simulations, scenarios, and environments, fostering experiential learning that transcends traditional boundaries. By immersing users in lifelike situations, VR and AR facilitate deep understanding and practical skill development, making complex concepts more tangible and memorable.

As we look into the realm of modern learning, it's crucial to recognize the significance of *adaptive learning systems*. These intelligent platforms leverage algorithms and data analytics to personalize the learning journey for each individual, catering to their unique strengths, weaknesses, and learning preferences. By dynamically adjusting content and pacing based on learner performance, adaptive learning ensures an optimized and personalized approach to skills development.

Modern learning techniques and tools have redefined the landscape of education and development, empowering individuals and organizations to embrace continuous learning in innovative ways. As we navigate this era of unprecedented change and complexity, leveraging these cutting-edge approaches will be instrumental in fostering a culture of lifelong learning and driving sustainable success.

Creating a Culture of Learning

Creating a culture of learning within an organization is essential for fostering continuous growth and development. A culture of learning encompasses the shared beliefs, values, and behaviors that prioritize and support ongoing learning and improvement at all levels. Such a culture encourages employees to seek out new knowledge, embrace innovative ideas, and engage in ongoing skill development. One of the fundamental elements of creating a culture of learning is *leadership commitment.* Leaders play a crucial role in shaping the environment where learning is valued and prioritized. When leaders demonstrate a commitment to their own learning and professional development, it sets a powerful example for others to follow. Organizations can create a culture of learning by promoting open communication and knowledge sharing. Encouraging collaboration and creating platforms for employees to exchange ideas and expertise helps to cultivate a rich learning environment.

Recognizing and rewarding a commitment to learning further reinforces the value of ongoing development. Another key aspect of creating a culture of learning is providing access to resources and opportunities for growth. *This can include investing in training programs, mentorship initiatives, and continuous learning platforms.* By offering access to these resources, organizations demonstrate their dedication to supporting employees in their pursuit of personal and professional advancement. It's also important to create a culture of psychological safety, where individuals feel comfortable taking risks, asking questions, and experimenting with new approaches without fear of judgment. This fosters an environment where learning and innovation thrive. Integrating learning into performance management processes and goal setting reinforces the importance of ongoing development as a core part of the organizational ethos. Overall, creating a culture of learning not only enhances individual performance and job satisfaction but also contributes to the long-term success and adaptability of the organization in an ever-evolving business landscape.

Overcoming Barriers to Learning

Learning is a perpetual journey, often filled with obstacles that can impede progress. Overcoming barriers to learning is essential for personal and professional growth. There are various challenges individuals and organizations encounter in the pursuit of continuous learning that need practical strategies to overcome them. One common barrier is the *lack of time*, as professionals juggle multiple responsibilities and commitments. To address this, *it is crucial to prioritize learning by allocating specific time slots for acquiring new knowledge and skills.* Another significant obstacle is *the fear of failure or making mistakes.*

Embracing a growth mindset and viewing failures as opportunities for learning can empower individuals to push past this mental barrier. *Limited access to resources and educational opportunities can hinder learning.* Organizations can support employees by providing access to online courses, workshops, and mentorship programs. A *lack of motivation or interest in learning* can also pose a challenge. Cultivating a culture of curiosity and emphasizing the relevance of continuous development to individual career success can inspire a proactive approach to learning.

Resistance to change within an organization can stifle the implementation of new learning initiatives. Leaders must communicate the benefits of ongoing learning and encourage open-mindedness among team members to mitigate resistance. *External factors such as financial constraints or family obligations may impact an individual's ability to dedicate time and resources to learning.* Employers can alleviate this barrier by offering flexible learning options and supporting work-life balance. By recognizing and addressing these barriers, individuals and organizations can foster an environment that promotes continuous learning and development, leading to enhanced performance and innovation.

Strategies for Self-Improvement
Continuous learning and development are vital for staying relevant and effective in a rapidly changing world. Below are the top five challenges related to continuous learning and development and strategies for overcoming them:

1. Finding Time for Learning
Challenge: Balancing the demands of work and personal life while finding time for continuous learning.

Self-Development Strategies:
Time Management:
- Time Blocking: Allocate specific blocks of time each week dedicated to learning. Treat these blocks as non-negotiable appointments.
- Prioritization: Use prioritization techniques, such as the Eisenhower Matrix, to identify and focus on high-priority learning activities.

Microlearning:
- *Short Sessions*: Incorporate microlearning by engaging in short, focused learning sessions (5-15 minutes) that can fit into your schedule.
- *Learning Apps*: Use learning apps that offer bite-sized lessons and on-the-go learning opportunities.

Integration into Daily Routine:
- *Learning During Commutes*: Utilize commuting time to listen to educational podcasts or audiobooks.
- *Lunch and Learn*: Participate in or organize lunch-and-learn sessions where you and your colleagues can learn new skills during lunch breaks.

2. Staying Motivated

Challenge: Maintaining motivation and commitment to continuous learning over the long term.

Self-Development Strategies:

Goal Setting:
- SMART Goals: Set SMART (Specific, Measurable, Achievable, Relevant, Time-bound) learning goals to stay focused and motivated.
- Milestones: Break down larger learning goals into smaller milestones to track progress and celebrate achievements.

Learning Communities:
- *Study Groups*: Join or form study groups with peers who share similar learning interests to stay motivated and accountable.
- *Online Forums*: Participate in online forums and communities related to your

learning interests to share knowledge and gain support.

Personal Interests:
- *Passion Projects*: Choose learning topics that genuinely interest and excite you to maintain intrinsic motivation.
- *Variety*: Incorporate variety in your learning activities to keep them engaging and prevent burnout.

3. Access to Resources

Challenge: Identifying and accessing high-quality learning resources and opportunities.

Self-Development Strategies:

Curating Resources:
- *Resource Lists*: Create curated lists of reputable books, online courses, podcasts, and other learning materials.
- *Library Memberships*: Join local or online libraries to access a wide range of learning resources.

Online Learning Platforms:
- *MOOCs*: Enroll in Massive Open Online Courses (MOOCs) offered by platforms like Coursera, edX, and Udacity to access high-quality courses from top institutions.

- *Webinars and Workshops*: Participate in webinars and virtual workshops to gain insights from industry experts.

Mentorship and Networking:
- *Mentors*: Seek out mentors who can provide guidance and recommend valuable learning resources.
- *Professional Associations*: Join professional associations related to your field to gain access to exclusive learning materials and events.

4. Applying Learned Knowledge

Challenge: Effectively applying new knowledge and skills in practical, real-world situations.

Self-Development Strategies:

Project-Based Learning:
- *Real Projects*: Apply new skills by working on real projects at work or through volunteer opportunities.
- *Simulations*: Participate in simulations or case studies to practice applying theoretical knowledge in realistic scenarios.

Reflective Practice:
- *Journaling*: Keep a learning journal to reflect on what you've learned and how you can apply it.
1. *After-Action Reviews*: Conduct after-action reviews to evaluate the effectiveness of applied knowledge and identify areas for improvement.

Feedback Mechanisms:
- *Peer Feedback*: Seek feedback from peers and mentors on how well you are applying new skills.
- *Self-Assessment*: Regularly assess your own performance and progress to identify gaps and areas for further development.

5. Keeping Up with Industry Changes

Challenge: Staying current with the latest developments, trends, and technologies in your industry.

Self-Development Strategies:

Continuous Monitoring:
- *Industry News*: Subscribe to industry news sources, journals, and newsletters to stay informed about the latest trends and developments.

- *Social Media*: Follow industry influencers and thought leaders on social media platforms to gain insights and updates.

Professional Development:
- *Certifications*: Pursue relevant certifications that keep you up-to-date with industry standards and best practices.
- *Conferences and Seminars*: Attend industry conferences, seminars, and trade shows to learn about the latest innovations and network with professionals.

Lifelong Learning Mindset:
- *Growth Mindset*: Cultivate a growth mindset by embracing continuous learning as a lifelong journey.
- *Adaptability*: Stay adaptable by being open to learning new skills and exploring different areas within your industry.

www.ingramcontent.com/pod-product-compliance
Lightning Source LLC
Chambersburg PA
CBHW052308220526
45472CB00001B/28